PUTTING

THE

PIECES

TOGETHER

D1287836

PUTTING THE PIECES TOGETHER

A SCRIPTURAL STUDY ON HOLINESS

LOUIE E. BUSTLE AND TED HUGHES

BEACON HILL PRESS
OF KANSAS CITY

Contents

Preface

The Bible is a book about holiness. It deals primarily with a holy God who wants to fellowship with a holy people and with the history of what He has done to make it possible. Holiness is at its very heart, and all its doctrines take their meaning from their relationship to its central theme.

The purpose of this writing is to help you put the puzzle pieces together, to help you see the big picture of God's provision for victorious Christian living in a postmodern world. Through 95 brief devotional readings on holiness—with scriptures taken from Genesis to Revelation—you will learn that a holiness lifestyle is available to you now.

There are several guiding principles. First, understanding the doctrine of holiness is a key to understanding the Bible. Second, the experience of holiness is for every believer. Third, holiness is not simply a doctrine among many others; rather it is *the unifying principle* of all doctrines.

The authors pray that you will not only grasp this truth intellectually but also be challenged to seek the experience through total consecration and the fullness of the Holy Spirit.

Introduction

The general theme of holiness is taught in different ways in the Bible.

- It begins in the creation story in Genesis.
- It is found in the Law of Moses.
- It is symbolized in Leviticus.
- It is illustrated in the history of Israel.
- It is beautified in the poetical books.
- It is diagrammed in the architecture of the Tabernacle and Temple.
- It is expressed in the proclamations of the prophets.
- It is revealed practically in the teachings of Jesus.
- It is explained fully in the letters of Paul and the other New Testament writers.

The Centrality of Holiness

These different ways to teach holiness are all parts of the same story. To get the whole story, we want to take a brief look at a wide panorama of Bible verses and their applications and to show how the scarlet thread of holiness runs throughout the Bible. It is hoped that the cumulative effect of the many verses will make you aware of the centrality of holiness. No effort has been made to organize them in a systematic way. They are simply presented in the order that they occur in the Bible. A study of the verse and a practical application will help you personalize these great truths.

The Puzzle Pieces

The method of this study of holiness is similar to the process of putting together a jigsaw puzzle. You open the box and dump the puzzle pieces into a shapeless heap. There is nothing attractive about the pile. But then, you pick up one piece at a time and try to figure out where it fits into the "picture." After a while, certain patterns and images begin to appear. And after the last piece is put into place, a beautiful, impressive picture is completed. None of the isolated pieces could even suggest the grandeur achieved when they all were put together in their proper relationships to each other.

The Complete Picture

The doctrine of holiness is similar. There are many pieces to it. Looking at only one piece does not reveal the glory of the complete picture. The beauty is revealed when they all come together. So, in this book, you will begin to pick up the pieces as concepts in scripture verses one at a time, seemingly at random. But as you proceed, the jumbled pieces gradually begin to take shape until the beautiful puzzle is complete.

God is the artist. He completed the masterwork one piece at a time—throughout history. Remember, every piece is important, but it is only as each piece is seen in its relationship to the total picture that its true beauty can be appreciated. That is why this book is titled *Putting the Pieces Together*.

Now we invite you to open the treasures of the Scriptures and lay out the verses and readings as you would a favorite puzzle. As you reflect on this book in a quiet time alone with God, the pieces will come together to make a beautiful portrait of His grace and power.

Have a great time of discovery, and enjoy the blessings as you apply them to your life.

LOUIE E. BUSTLE AND TED HUGHES

Wesleyan Teaching on Entire Sanctification

After a careful study of the Scriptures and human experience, John Wesley concluded that full salvation involves two steps in which God intervenes in a work of grace in the human heart. The first is *regeneration* (the new birth), *justification* (a right relationship to God's law), and adoption into the family of God. All of these occur simultaneously and deal with forgiveness for committed acts of sin and the resulting guilt.

The second work is *entire sanctification*, which deals with the sinful nature (original or inherited sin), and requires cleansing by the Holy Spirit. This is what the disciples experienced when they were baptized with the Holy Spirit and fire on the Day of Pentecost (Acts 15:9).

Filled with the Spirit

The experience of cleansing is available by faith to all born-again believers who reach a point of complete consecration to God. Simultaneously, the Holy Spirit "fills" the believers completely and in greater measure. His indwelling presence enables or empowers the person for a victorious life and service to God.

Wesley also made a clear distinction between heart purity and Christian maturity. The first is an act of the Holy Spirit, which happens in a moment of time. The latter is a growth process that goes on throughout life. We develop a Christlike character through discipline and learning.

Many Terms, One Work

This cleansing work of God's grace is also known by other terms, such as:
- Entire sanctification
- Christian perfection
- Perfect love
- Heart purity

- Baptism with the Holy Spirit
- Second work of grace
- Second blessing
- Christian holiness
- Full salvation
- Filled with the Spirit

Whichever term you may use, as a believer, the work is the same. In answer to prayer and through faith in God's promised provision, He cleanses your heart of the carnal nature that rebels against His will; the sanctifying work of Christ is applied as you consecrate your life to Him; you are completely filled with the Holy Spirit, resulting in perfect love; and you are empowered to live a life of loving obedience. As a glorious bonus, the Holy Spirit gives personal assurance to this work of grace in your heart.

For the apostle Paul, all Christians are called to become what they are in Christ through the Spirit. In other words, God invites all to become His holy people. And this invitation is for now, not just for the future.

Essential of Wesleyan Theology

Beliefs are subject to human tweaking. The holiness emphasis was preached with power during the 18th century, but the next century's proclamation of the doctrine had its own interpretations. The bottom line is that God's purpose and plan for a holy people transcend all generations—and human tweaking.

Here we will briefly focus on a few essential points in Wesleyan theology.

Entire sanctification is a second work of grace. It happens after a person has been born again, which is a necessary step in preparation for entire sanctification. A sinful life or a sinful nature cannot be consecrated to God.

Entire sanctification is received instantaneously. There is a process that will lead up to the experience and a process that will follow it. But when the Holy Spirit does the act of cleansing—since it is a faith experience—it happens in a moment of time.

Entire sanctification deals with the problem of the sinful nature. In this act we are purified from the sinful nature. The sinful nature manifests itself as an inclination toward sinning, a false sense of personal sovereignty, and self-centeredness.

Entire sanctification is attainable in this life. Since sanctification is clearly taught in the Bible, all theologies must find a place for it. Some schools of thought place it at the moment of death or between death and heaven, and so forth. The Bible teaches that it is the grace of sanctification that prepares us for living a victorious life in this world as well as to prepare us for the world to come.

Entire sanctification and the baptism with the Holy Spirit are simultaneous. This is the experience the disciples had on the Day of Pentecost when their hearts were "purified by faith."*

---

*The outline for these first five points is taken from Stephen S. White, *Five Cardinal Elements in the Doctrine of Entire Sanctification* (Kansas City: Beacon Hill Press, 1948).

Holiness is commanded. It is not an optional grace. It is the only way that we can please God (Heb. 12:14).

Holiness is God's will for us. He wants to sanctify us and will respond to all who sincerely seek this grace and pay the price of a complete consecration to Him (1 Thess. 4:3).

A holy heart is a requirement for entrance into heaven. It is not optional. The only "exceptions" are those who have been genuinely converted and are walking in all the light they have up to that time. While the Bible states, "Without holiness no one will see the Lord" (Heb. 12:14), it also states, "If we walk in the light as He is in the light . . . the blood of Jesus Christ His Son cleanses us from all sin" (1 John 1:7, NKJV). The command to be holy should be understood in its relationship to "walking in the light." Even after cleansing we must continue to walk in the light to maintain a holy life.

Holiness in the Old Testament

In the Old Testament, much of the teaching about holiness is in the form of ceremonies and rituals that were types of the realities to come. Cleansing, for example, was only ceremonial and foreshadowed the future ministry of the Holy Spirit. The teaching of Christ and the experience of the apostles at Pentecost greatly amplified and clarified the shadows of the Old Testament. The apostolic writings gave deeper insight into what had been mysteries.

We can learn a lot about holiness from the rules for worship as given in Leviticus. While much of it had to do with ceremony and ritual, they were like simple object lessons containing important truth. Some of it had to do with the consecration and care of objects and utensils used in the Temple worship. These rules defined the objects as holy or unholy, clean or unclean. In the New Testament these same concepts would be applied to people.

For example, to be considered worthy to be used in worship, an object had to be separated from common use and set apart completely for sacred use. It had to be washed and kept spotlessly clean. If perchance it became contaminated, elaborate rituals were required to cleanse it before it could be used again. This is the primitive and foreshadowing form of total consecration and cleansing in the New Testament.

Some of the teaching was prophetic. Prophets like Jeremiah, Ezekiel, and Joel were given insights into truth centuries before events actually happened.

A lot about holiness was contained in the Law. However, it must be remembered that there are various categories of the Law, each given for different purposes, and that these diverse types of the law do not all have equal weight. For example, there was the ceremonial law, which was temporary. Jesus would later fulfill it and make it no longer necessary. There were civil laws governing the political functions of the nation at that time. The Law even contained instructions concerning the health and hygiene of a nomadic people who had special needs as they lived in the desert. They had no refrigeration and knew little about proper cooking as well as the dangers and spoilage of specific foods. Then there was the moral law as typified by the Ten Commandments. The moral law deals with absolute principles that will never change or become outdated. The specific teachings about holiness are in this category.

All of the Old Testament teaching about holiness is directed to the future. It was all preparatory for something to come. It dealt with only shadows and symbols of a reality that was not yet available, but in due time would be fulfilled. It was a very preliminary part of God's plan, but it did give hope as to where the plan of God was headed.

The full glory of the experience would be more adequately revealed in the New Testament, but it would be based on the fulfillment of the foundation laid in the Old Testament centuries before.

1

God's Purpose from the Beginning

So God created man in his own image, in the image of God he created him; male and female he created them. —Gen. 1:27

Let's start from the beginning. Isn't it interesting that in the first chapter of the Bible God lays out so clearly what His design was for humankind? Actually, it had been determined long before the creative act (see Eph. 1:4).

God had a plan and it was related to His purpose for the creation of this new and unique creature He called "man" and "woman." God wanted to enjoy the love, fellowship, and service of another free being like himself.

The only way this could be accomplished was if this new

creature would share some of the characteristics of God himself. Since God was a (divine) person, human beings were granted personhood: the ability to think and reason (intellect), feel (emotion), and make choices (free will). But this was not enough because persons can relate to each other in tension and conflict. God wanted to be in harmony with people, so He shared His own nature (holy) with them. This should not seem strange since even on the human level the deepest and most intimate levels of fellowship can only be achieved between two persons who share similar interests and values.

When the time arrived to carry out God's plan, the Bible summarized it by saying that God "created man in his own image." That is to say, He created human beings in many respects like himself: as persons to have possible interaction with another person (God); as a spirit to facilitate communication between spirits; holy, to ensure harmony with God's holiness; and free, to make love and service voluntary.

God's design for us can never change! What He wants for us and from us will always be the same. Unfortunately, sin intervened and frustrated the original plan, but God's wonderful plan of redemption has the specific purpose of restoring human beings to their original place in God's design.

Question for Reflection: Do you have a genuine hunger to be like God?

2

Blamelessness

Noah was a righteous man, blameless among the people of his time, and he walked with God.

—Gen. 6:9

What a disappointment Adam's and Eve's sin must have been to God! He had created the human race with so much potential. But His expectation of a relationship of love and fellowship had not turned out that way. The misuse of the freedom God had given led to disobedience and rebellion. By this time almost the entire human race had turned against Him. The entire world was full of corruption, wickedness, and violence.

Conditions on earth were so bad that God was sorry He had created the human race, and "his heart was filled with pain" (v. 6). The only solution seemed to be to wipe out humankind and start all over again.

However, you may have noticed that it was stated above that "almost the entire race" had turned against Him. There was an exception, a man whose name was Noah, the only person in the whole world with whom God was pleased. The comment about him is that he was righteous and blameless, and that he "walked with God." These comments seem to indicate that he alone had fulfilled the purposes for which the race was created. He evidently was blameless (without guilt) because he obeyed God's commandments. The fact that he "walked with God" implies fellowship and harmony.

This is remarkable in the light of the universal moral degeneration of the society around him. It is positive proof that it is possible to live a righteous life even when subjected to incredibly negative influences.

Noah refused to let the wicked world around him squeeze him into its mold. It is never easy to go against the current. It takes courage, strength, and firm resolve, but Noah proved it could be done.

If Noah could do it, so can you!

Question for Reflection: In what ways have you allowed the world to influence your thoughts and actions?

3

Perfect or Blameless?

Noah was a righteous man, blameless among the
people of his time, and he walked with God.

—Gen. 6:9

Is it possible to live a perfect life?

In the King James Version of the Bible, there are a number
of texts where the word "perfect" is either applied to a living
human being or is used as a description or a command concerning a person's relationship to God. In reaction against the idea of
absolute perfection, which pertains only to God, and the confusion resulting from it, the *New International Version* has substitut-
ed the word "blameless" in place of "perfect." Which is right?

A quick look at the dictionary gives the following defini-
tions of "perfect": "Complete in all respects; without defects;
flawless; pure; without reserve or qualification."* In the light of
many biblical texts, these qualities may legitimately apply to
the relationship that God seeks and expects from His children.
Is it not possible to please God in such a way that He is satisfied with the relationship? Is it not possible to love Him without defects or flaws in our love? Is it not possible to consecrate
ourselves to Him without reserve or qualification? Is it not possible for a person and God to enter into a mutually satisfactory
relationship? If it is a relationship that meets the desires and
expectations of both parties, is it not a perfect relationship?

On the other hand, what does the word blameless mean?
To blame someone is to make an accusation against the person;
to condemn; to find fault. To be blameless indicates that the
person is not guilty of any accusation; is not condemned for
any reason; and no fault is found. Used in this way, it is a satisfactory relationship.

Both the words "blameless" and "perfect" should be

Webster's New World Dictionary, 2nd ed., 1986.

acceptable if we understand their meaning and do not let either of them dilute the kind of relationship God seeks with His children. He realizes that we will never reach absolute perfection, but He does seek a deep, intimate relation of love and devotion that is complete and leaves no room for flaws as far as the intentions of our hearts are concerned.

Question for Reflection: What word best describes your relationship with God?

4

The Standard for God's People

When Abram was ninety-nine years old, the Lord appeared to him and said, "I am God Almighty; walk before me and be blameless."   —Gen. 17:1

God sets high standards for His people. In this case "blameless" means consistent obedience, no disobedience, no willful sinning, no unfaithfulness, no excuses.

It is clear that God wants us to maintain a continuous correct relationship with Him. His desire is that we avoid an off-again-on-again love for Him as it was for a good part of Israel's history. Part-time love and obedience are not acceptable.

There is no excuse for the sin of disobedience. Nobody has to sin—ever. Habitual sin must be abandoned as a requirement for justification. Adequate provisions have been made to enable us to resist temptation. It is true that provision has been made for forgiveness for a Christian who has fallen into sin in a moment of weakness, but that is not the norm for the Christian life. God's norm for His disciples is that we walk before Him and be blameless.

God's grace has the wonderful possibility of keeping us in an unbroken relationship of love and fellowship. It is also possible to live a life of victory over sin and the condemnation that results from it. All the resources we need to achieve it are available to us.

It is unwise for a Christian to look for loopholes to get around God's laws or to settle for less than the victory that Christ died to give us. Any "salvation" that leaves us still in sin is unworthy of a holy God who hates sin. All of God's works are characterized by excellence and generosity. His work of redemption is complete, efficacious, and glorious. It is not a weak measure that does not solve the problem. It is powerful medicine that leads to complete deliverance.

It is a dangerous practice to see how close we can get to sin without falling into it. It is better to give it the widest possible avoidance.

Question for Reflection: Is there any thought or habit in your life that comes dangerously close to disobedience?

5

God's Promises Are Conditional

Now if you obey me fully and keep my covenant, then out of all nations you will be my treasured possession. Although the whole earth is mine, you will be for me a kingdom of priests and a holy nation.
—Exod. 19:5–6*a*

One of the best things about God is that He is always faithful. He never lies, He's always on time, and His promises are always true! Yet sometimes there is a condition placed on receiving God's promise. We receive good things from Him when certain conditions are met.

In this passage, God gives Moses an important message for the Israelites. He has a special plan for them. It has been in operation for some time since He brought them out of Egypt. The memory of God's actions in their behalf on the past should be a source of encouragement as they look toward the future. God wants to do great things for them and through them.

But wait! There is one small word of great significance in the text: "Now if you obey me fully and keep my covenant . . ." It is a conditional offer. The fulfillment of the promised blessings depends on the "if." The phrase following "if" is the condition on which the promise rests. God's promises are always that way. There is something we must do first to qualify for the promise. Two conditions are established here: (1) full obedience, and (2) faithfulness to the covenant. Now, look at the key phrases in the promised blessings.

"You will be my treasured possession." What wonderful things are implied in that phrase. Of all the people of the world, those who meet the conditions will be God's favorites. They will be the focus of God's special attention.

"You will be to me a kingdom of priests." In the Old Testament, the priests had special access to God. They were the chosen ones through whom God worked to accomplish His purposes. They were the mediators between God and humankind. What a privilege!

"A holy nation." From the beginning it was clear that God's people, individually and collectively, are to be holy. There is no substitute for holiness in God's people. They must be consecrated and cleansed to participate in His mission to the world.

Question for Reflection: Have you placed yourself in a position to receive good things from God?

6

The Basis of Our Fellowship with God

You are to be my holy people.   —Exod. 22:31

"What does God want for me?" Many people ask a question like that one, trying to determine God's will for their lives. In fact, God's will for us is very simple: He wants us to be like Him. He wants us to be holy.

The Bible clearly states, in both the Old and the New Testaments, that His desire and command for His people is to be holy. We understand that the definition of "holy" in the New Testament has a deeper meaning and application, but even its use in the Old Testament is very significant. When applied to things, it meant they were set apart for sacred uses. They were consecrated for special purposes. Through elaborate rituals they were ceremonially kept clean from contamination. Holy things were in a different category from common things.

In the course of time, it came to be understood that the word "holy" could also be applied to people. God's people are also to be set apart; they are to be different from other people, and they are to be cleansed and kept clean.

"Holy" is the same word God uses in the New Testament to describe himself. It is the only word that comprehensibly describes the complete nature of God. Being the same word that describes the nature of God and God's ideal for us, it makes sense that to be holy is to be godly. Here we have one of the most amazing facts of God's self-disclosure: His plan is to allow us to participate in His nature in such a way that it becomes the basis of intimate fellowship and harmony with Him.

This should be the ultimate goal of our striving. It is the highest achievement attainable to a human being. This is what is so amazing about grace. A sinful, depraved person can rise to the level of godliness through grace.

God did not wait for the New Testament to reveal His desire for human beings. He was up-front about it from the very beginning. Nothing could ever substitute for holiness. It took some time for the full provision of this truth to become complete, but God's desire for us has always been the same.

Question for Reflection: Are you pursuing God's vision for your life or your own vision?

7

The Holy Sabbath

> You must observe my Sabbaths. This will be a sign between me and you for the generations to come, so you may know that I am the LORD, who makes you holy.   —Exod. 31:13

What is the most important thing in your life? Without knowing anything about you, I can probably identify what that is. It is whatever occupies the greatest share of your time and attention—it is what you worship.

In this passage, the subject is worship—specifically Sabbath observance. It's important to understand that in the context of these verses, Moses is giving detailed instructions for the Tabernacle, its furniture, the ark, altars, priestly garments, and decorations. It was a place where God would meet in a special way with His worshippers. It was not intended to be a museum. All of its contents were designed to be aids in the act of worship. Then God says, "You must observe my Sabbaths." In other words, the Tabernacle with all of its contents would be useless unless worship actually took place there. The Tabernacle was only the equipment to facilitate worship, not worship itself.

Here God singles out Sabbath observance as one of His most important commands. The regular worship of God's people is the practice that will have a profound influence on future generations. Everything spiritual will be weakened and begin to fall apart if the Sabbath is neglected.

It is through the correct observance of the Sabbath that we learn who God is and what He does. The sovereignty and Lordship of God is recognized in regular worship. And, through it all, God's purpose is to make us holy. There is no other way for a person to become holy. Only God can do that! So much energy is wasted trying to get around that fact and achieve it by our own efforts. New resolutions and efforts to improve one's behavior are doomed to failure. People have learned to do many things by human strength and knowledge, but only God can change the sinful nature. He does it only after He has been recognized as Lord.

It is extremely important for God's people to get into the habit of worshipping Him regularly. The proper observance of the Sabbath will have an impact on future generations. In our day, we need to develop anew a reverence for God's special day.

Question for Reflection: What occupies most of your time and attention?

8

The Seal of God's Kingdom

They made the plate, the sacred diadem, out of pure gold and engraved on it, like an inscription on a seal: HOLY TO THE LORD. —Exod. 39:30

When you belong to a team, you wear a uniform that signifies your membership in the group. And when you own something, you usually place some identifying mark upon it. Your car is probably registered in your name. You may inscribe your name on the inside of a book that you own. If you are married, you may wear a wedding ring that signifies that you belong to someone else. How does it feel to know that God has placed His seal of ownership upon you as one of His people?

Moses gave detailed instructions for the preparation of the garments to be worn by the priests as they ministered in the Tabernacle. A part of their "uniform" was a plate made of pure gold inscribed with the words "HOLY TO THE LORD." It was like the official seal or badge of a government that identified and gave authority to the wearer. In a similar way, the badge on a police uniform symbolizes the authority of the entity the officer represents. Or, it could be thought of as an official government seal affixed to a document that attests its genuineness. At any rate, it is significant that holiness is the key concept on the seal chosen to identify the agents of God's kingdom on earth. Holiness is the concept most identified with the kingdom of God.

To this day the inscription on that seal appears on the church buildings, official seals, and letterheads of Holiness denominations. It seems appropriate because it is what the Christian message is all about. Holiness is not a peripheral message. It is the central theme of the Bible. In a nutshell, the theme of the Bible is about a holy God who wants a holy people and what He has done to make it possible. It is inconceivable that the word "holy" could be removed from the Bible. No other word so comprehensibly describes the nature of God. It is His desire for human beings, the requirement to enter His presence, and His standard for human conduct.

The holiness of God is a central concept in our worship. We worship God because He is holy. Our music and our praise ascribe holiness to Him. We sing heartily, "Holiness unto the Lord now and forever!" We are moved to a spirit of reverence when we sing, "Holy, Holy, Holy!"

The inscription on the seal of the Kingdom is very significant because it establishes holiness as the central concept on which the Kingdom is established. It is not an exaggeration to say that in summary the Bible is a book about holiness. Everything in the Bible is in some way related to holiness. This is especially true of doctrines based on the Bible. You can start to expound any biblical doctrine and it will eventually lead you to holiness. This is because ultimately all doctrines are related to holiness and because ultimately all doctrine arises from the nature of God. It can be illustrated by a wagon wheel in which the spokes represent different doctrines, but they are all tied together in the hub, which is holiness, as illustrated on the next page.

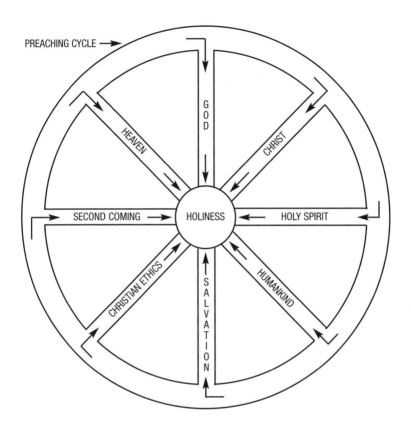

Examples

God: God is holy, and He wants us to be holy.

Christ: Christ suffered to make the Church holy.

Holy Spirit: His baptism is a purifying baptism of fire.

Humankind: Our greatest need is to be restored to holiness.

Salvation: Salvation is only complete when the sinful nature is cleansed.

Christian Ethics: The biblical standard is to live a holy life.

Second Coming: The only way to be prepared is to live a godly life.

Heaven: Nothing impure will ever enter heaven.

Question for Reflection: Is the word "holy" inscribed upon your heart?

9

Clean and Unclean

You must distinguish between the holy and the common, between the unclean and the clean.
—Lev. 10:10

God had a problem. He wanted to reveal His plan of salvation to sinful people, but it would not be easy because He had to penetrate minds that were dulled and darkened by the effects of sin. It would be like trying to teach calculus to a kindergartner. It would take a long time and would have to start at a very low level of understanding. Much like schoolteachers, God would have to resort to simple object lessons to accommodate the limitations of His students.

This is what the Book of Leviticus is about. God instituted a system of symbols, types, and visual aids to help humankind understand its pitiful condition and the need for change.

Now, where did God start? At the simplest level, of course: By calling to humankind's attention that there is a difference between what is clean and what is not. So much depends on being able to distinguish between the two!

Sin is represented in the Bible as contamination. Human beings were not created in that condition, but when sin entered the race it contaminated the very nature of humankind. Something beautiful was lost: innocence, purity, cleanness, holiness. However, it was God's plan to open the door to the recovery of what was lost. The first step in that direction was to make people aware of the loss. It involved seeing sin as uncleanness in contrast to the holiness of God. The recognition of our uncleanness would lead to a consciousness of our need for cleansing. Once we understood the problem, it would be an incentive to seeking a solution. It is so much better to be clean than to be contaminated. We can be thankful that God has provided a complete solution to the pollution of sin.

Think about it. If God had not gone to extreme measures

to teach us the difference between clean and unclean, we would never have known the difference.

Question for Reflection: Are you aware of any areas in your life that need to be cleansed?

10

Why Be Holy?

> I am the LORD your God; consecrate yourselves and be holy, because I am holy. Do not make yourselves unclean . . . I am the LORD who brought you up out of Egypt to be your God; therefore be holy, because I am holy.
> —Lev. 11:44-45

Whenever God gives us a command, there is a reason behind it. We don't serve an arbitrary, capricious God who makes demands of us for no reason. Instead, we have a Heavenly Father who loves us and is eager to see us experience good things. That's why God gave us the command to be holy—because He loves us!

Many false concepts have been advanced for this command to be holy. Some see God as a tyrant who wants to enslave us into obedience to a bunch of rules He has arbitrarily invented. Others may see holiness as a form of punishment that takes the "fun" out of life. But here God makes it very plain that the reason behind the command is simply that He wants us to be like Him. Why does God want that? Because He seeks intimate fellowship with us! This can only happen where there is a commonality of thinking, values, spirit, and nature. Where these are antagonistic, unity and harmony are destroyed and intimate fellowship is impossible.

This desire on the part of God is generated by His love for us. He wants to bless us, and He always knows what is in our best interest. He will never deprive us of anything that in the long run would be good for us. He always acts in our favor, never against us. He wants us to know Him in all the beauty and splendor of His holiness. The greatest gift He can give us is to share His nature with us. What wondrous love!

We usually think of this experience as the New Testament standard of Christian experience, but it has been the goal ever since the beginning. True, a lot took place between the time Moses first said it and the time Peter reiterated it (1 Pet. 1:15). God's self-disclosure had advanced and had become clearer since its perfection in His Son, but likeness to His nature has always been His goal.

Question for Reflection: How do you view God's commandments—as rules to obey or as a pathway to life?

11

Consecrate and Sanctify

"Consecrate yourselves and be holy."   —Lev. 11:44*a*
"I am the LORD, who makes you holy."   —Lev. 20:8*b*

In the process of becoming holy, there is something you can do and something else that only God can do. The first is called *consecration.* The second is *sanctification.* These two verses demonstrate the difference. In the first text above we are urged to consecrate ourselves, while in the second text it is stated that it is "the LORD, who makes you holy" (emphasis added). Consecration is the human side of the equation; sanctification is the divine response. Consecration is the condition that makes it possible for God to sanctify. Consecration must always precede entire sanctification.

Some people have been attracted to sanctification and have tried to achieve it by trying to "do better" or "try harder." This method simply does not work, for it is based on human effort. Only God can make us holy! God clearly states that making human beings holy is a part of His job description. To move from unholy to holy requires a cleansing by faith that only God can do.

On the other hand, God cannot do His work until we meet the condition, which is consecration. Consecration means to submit to God's will and give Him permission to "make us holy." The goal is complete consecration. That is, giving ourselves to God without reservation. When that happens it allows the Holy Spirit to enter in His fullness and take control without limitation. At this point our hearts are purified, fellowship with God is deepened, our usefulness to God is increased, and our spiritual growth is accelerated.

We need to concentrate on the consecration. God is faithful and will always do His part when He sees that we are ready. If you have been seeking holiness and God has not responded, ask Him to show you what the problem is. You do not have to persuade Him to sanctify you. He already wants to do it (see Luke 11:13). You simply need to give Him permission and make sure there is nothing about you that prevents Him from doing the work of grace. If you sincerely seek, He will show you where the problem is.

Question for Reflection: Are you doing "your part" by consecrating yourself completely to God?

12

Love at the Center

Love the LORD your God with all your heart and with all your soul and with all your strength.   —Deut. 6:5

What is it that God really wants from me? He doesn't need my advice because His wisdom is limitless. He doesn't need my help because He can do anything He wants. What He really wants is my love.

What kind of love is it that God is looking for? It is not a superficial love that He wants. The Bible describes it in extreme terms as seen in the verse above. It is a love that involves the totality of our being; a love that is exclusive; a love that gives Him top priority; a love that surpasses our love for anything or anybody else; a love without flaw; a love from a free being who chooses to love Him. (Love from a free being is the only thing God could not create, and that is why He gave us the capacity to love and the freedom to choose.) Love is not a feeling; it is a choice.

This special kind of love is the essence of holiness. John Wesley had it right when he said, "Holiness is nothing more or less than loving God with the whole heart, soul, mind, and strength." That kind of love implies total commitment. It fulfills the demands of complete consecration. Consecration is not giving ourselves to God grudgingly: it is an act of love. It meets all of God's requirements. What more could we give than our total, all-embracing, supreme love and devotion? Loving God more than anything else is the essence of total consecration.

We usually think of this kind of love as a New Testament standard. But there it is in Deut. 6. It is what God has wanted all along. There is no substitute for it.

If we love God enough, we would never think of disobeying Him or doing anything that would displease Him. If we love Him enough, our sole purpose in life is to do His will and to live for His glory.

Question for Reflection: Do you have a pure love for God?

13

A Matter of the Heart

The LORD your God will circumcise your hearts and the hearts of your descendants, so that you may love him with all your heart and with all your soul, and live."   —Deut. 30:6

Wearing a uniform doesn't make you a policeman any

more than wearing a ring makes you married. In both cases, the outer symbol is intended to represent something deeper—the essence of the person on the inside.

It is the same with circumcision, the outer sign God instituted to identify the people of His covenant. However, the Jews did not fully understand the meaning of the symbol. In the course of time, they became very legalistic about it. The symbol became more important than the truth it was meant to symbolize. God's covenant with Israel was more than a physical act performed by human hands. It represented a spiritual relationship that involved the heart. As this became more evident, the biblical writers began to speak of it as "circumcision of the heart" in both the Old and New Testaments.

This new consciousness focuses on several important facts: Christianity is not a matter of ritual or liturgy; it is a matter of the heart. You cannot claim to be a Christian simply by signing a card, reciting a creed, or having your name entered on a denominational roll. Even baptism is not a guarantee of salvation. It is the reality behind the symbol that counts.

Circumcision of the heart implies a change of nature. It means cutting away the "flesh" of the old sinful nature and replacing it with a new spiritual nature.

Please note that God follows through to explain why it is necessary. He does it "so that you may love him with all your heart and with all your soul, and live." It is impossible to love Him to this degree while the sinful nature still dominates the heart. It takes a change of heart to enable us to love God in this way. The true Jew as well as the true Christian is the one who has undergone radical heart surgery performed by the divine hand of the Holy Spirit. Outward symbols do not count for much with God unless there is a corresponding reality in the heart.

Question for Reflection: Are you in reality the way you present yourself to others?

14

Consecration Leads to Amazing Things

Joshua told the people, "Consecrate yourselves, for tomorrow the LORD will do amazing things among you." —Josh. 3:5

Consecration and heart holiness go hand in hand. In fact, they are inseparable. None of us can hope to become holy without first consecrating ourselves to God. Let's look at some of the reasons for that.

God will work this wonder only in the life of a person over whom He has complete control. Any lack of consecration puts a limitation on God to that same degree. He will only lead a person into the fullness of His blessings where there is a complete disposition to fully obey Him. There is no such thing as partial obedience with God. To Him, that's the same as disobedience.

Consecration reaches its climax in a surrender of the will. It is more than a willingness to do certain things. It is more like signing a contract at the bottom of a blank page and letting God fill in the details. It is following the example of Christ in the garden when He prayed, "Not my will, but thine, be done" (Luke 22:42, KJV).

Consecration always precedes the "amazing things" that God does, like miraculously opening a path across the Red Sea. Consecration comes first, and then the marvelous works of God follow. We sometimes want to reverse the order and try to negotiate with God by offering to serve Him if He will first give us the miracle we want. It doesn't work that way.

Complete consecration, with no limitations or restrictions, is the absolute prerequisite to victorious Christian living. When we give up ourselves, we gain much more.

Question for Reflection: Are you trying to get the best from God while holding back a part of yourself?

15

God Will Not Tolerate Sin

Go, consecrate the people. Tell them, "Consecrate your-selves in preparation for tomorrow; for this is what the LORD, the God of Israel, says: That which is devoted is among you, O Israel. You cannot stand against your enemies until you remove it." —Josh. 7:13

There is no "secret" sin as far as God is concerned. He sees it all. Nothing can be hidden from Him. That's what the Israelites discovered after their great victory at Jericho.

Here's what had happened: God had promised the Israelites victory over their enemies in the conquest of Canaan. However, all of the plunder from their victories was to be devoted to the Lord and was to go into the treasury of the Tabernacle. But a man named Achan secretly took a few items of the plunder and buried it under his tent. When the Israelites later went into battle, they suffered a great loss. God then informed them that He could not continue to bless them until the situation was corrected. The sin of Achan was discovered, and he was severely punished. The experience was intended to be an important lesson for Israel.

Sin is a serious thing and must be dealt with in a radical way. It must not be taken lightly. The effects of sin may go far beyond the sinner himself or herself and have a painful result on many other innocent people.

Just as it did with the Israelites, sin will also rob us of vic-tory. We cannot expect to enjoy God's blessing while clinging to sin. In our quest for holiness, we must be completely obedi-ent to God and not try to keep even a few things hidden. There is no way to escape the consequences of sin. "You may be sure that your sin will find you out" (Num. 32:23).

Question for Reflection: Is there anything hidden in your life, from you or from God?

16

Full Commitment

> But your hearts must be fully committed to the LORD
> our God, to live by his decrees and obey his com-
> mands. —1 Kings 8:61

"But" is a tiny word that carries large implications. A
grammarian would call it an adversative conjunction. You and
I know it signals an important condition or contradiction. That
is never more true than in the verse at hand.

Solomon had completed the construction of the Temple
with all of its ornate details. The ark of the covenant had been
brought into the building and placed in the most holy place.
The time had arrived to dedicate the Temple. As part of the
ceremony, Solomon prayed a long, eloquent prayer of dedica-
tion as he knelt before the altar of the Lord with his hands
spread out toward heaven. Then he stood and faced the con-
gregation to present a challenge and pronounce a blessing
upon them. What a thrilling moment it was! Then, just before
he finished, he used that powerful little word—"but." All the
previous words of promise, blessings, and potential depended
on that one small, three-letter word, as Solomon went on to
say. "But your hearts must be fully committed to the LORD our
God, to live by his decrees and obey his commands."

No halfhearted measures, no lukewarm commitment, no
superficial obedience would do! Nothing less than being
"fully committed" to God's decrees and laws would be acceptable.

Isn't it amazing how many New Testament concepts are
found in seed form in the Old Testament? God's basic desires
and plans for humankind have never changed. Yes, it did take
a few millennia for these concepts to come to their full understanding. But in the light of a more perfect revelation, God still
wants the same thing He has always wanted: complete devotion and commitment to Him. He makes it clear that it is not a

ritualistic exercise or a repetition of mere words. It must come from the heart!

As in the Old Testament, there is still today a "but" following God's promises of blessing. He will not hesitate to give you the blessings, but your heart must be fully committed to Him. Start with a full consecration, and you will see the wonders of His response. Your full commitment to Him will bring His full commitment to you. That's a good deal: all of you for all of Him.

Question for Reflection: Are you willing to accept the condition of receiving God's blessing—full surrender to Him?

17

Consecration Must Be Maintained

> As Solomon grew old, his wives turned his heart
> after other gods, and his heart was not fully devoted
> to the LORD his God, as the heart of David his father
> had been.   —1 Kings 11:4

Prosperity can be a curse as well as a blessing. Perhaps you have discovered that it can be most difficult to follow God when our lives are the most comfortable. That was precisely the experience of Solomon, a man who had many advantages and opportunities and did many good things. Yet his life ended on a sad note.

In the early years of his reign he was granted wisdom, but later he made some foolish mistakes that led to his moral downfall, and even to idolatry. His story serves as a somber warning for all of us. He made the mistake of marrying wives from the pagan nations around Israel. He had been warned of the danger involved, but political expediency triumphed over divine guidance. The problem was that these pagan women brought with them their pagan religions, and Solomon felt obligated to tolerate them. His wives turned his heart after other gods, and his heart was not fully devoted to God.

It is impossible to be "fully devoted" to more than one thing at a time. Our God demands complete loyalty and will not share His worship with others.

There are many things that compete for God's attention in our lives. These things can become "gods" to us. It is always dangerous to tolerate their presence.

As with Solomon, it is not how we begin our journey with God but how we finish it that counts. Remember the words of Jesus: "Because of the increase of wickedness, the love of most will grow cold, but he who stands firm to the end will be saved" (Matt. 24:12–13).

Question for Reflection: What competes for God's attention in your life?

18

The Beauty of Holiness

Ascribe to the LORD the glory due his name. Bring an offering and come before him; worship the LORD in the splendor of his holiness.   —1 Chron. 16:29

What is the most beautiful thing in the world? To some, it might be a beautiful sunset or a stunning landscape. Others might say it is the face of their spouse or their children. There are many beautiful things in the world, but one surpasses them all— the holiness of God. Surely nothing could surpass the beauty of God himself, the Creator of all things beautiful. The blazing brightness of His glory is too great for human eyes to behold.

Amazingly, we are invited to come before this awesome God and worship in the splendor of His holiness. What a privilege! Each one of His attributes outshines the brightness of the sun. Taken together, these characteristics are what make Him a *holy* God. That is the term that God himself uses to describe His nature. His glory goes beyond the capacity of what even the most expressive words can describe.

Yet, wonder of wonders, in the New Testament we are informed that God wants us to become "partakers of the divine nature" (2 Pet. 1:4, NKJV). He wants to share His nature with the creatures He has created. That is actually the greatest gift He could bestow on humankind.

From that, it is easy to deduce that holiness is attractive, desirable, and good for us. It is the source of true joy and maximum blessing. How sad it is that the popular opinion is the opposite: that holiness is distasteful and will spoil the "fun" that life offers.

There is an inherent stand-alone beauty in holiness: it is the beauty of purity, love, peace, and harmony. It is all brought into focus in the act of worship as the human encounters the divine. They share a common nature; they share heart purity; they have a mutual commitment to each other, and they are pledged to a mutual love forever. They think the same way and share the same values. They enter into in-depth communion and enjoy each other's presence. It is beautiful: the beauty of holiness.

Question for Reflection: How well do you know this holy God?

19

Carry Out the Rubbish

Listen to me, Levites! Consecrate yourselves now and consecrate the temple of the LORD, the God of your fathers. Remove all defilement [NKJV, "rubbish"] from the sanctuary.   —2 Chron. 29:5

Nobody likes garbage. We haul it away from our homes

and do what we can to keep them spotlessly clean. How much more should we be interested in removing the junk from our hearts? That's the lesson we learn from this scripture.

There was a time when activity in the Temple was the heart and soul of Israel, but over time it had fallen into neglect. They had "trespassed and done evil in the eyes of the LORD; . . . turned their faces away from the dwelling place of the LORD, and turned their backs on Him" (v. 6, NKJV).

The doors of the Temple had been closed; the lamps had been extinguished, and the burning of incense and the offerings to God had ceased. It was truly a sad situation. Picture it in your mind if you can. Dust and dirt and all sorts of filthiness had filtered in. Spider webs were everywhere. Rubbish was strewn around on the floors. What a mess!

Enter Hezekiah. He was appalled. He started by opening the doors and repairing them. Then he ordered the Levites to "sanctify the house of the LORD God of your fathers, and carry out the rubbish from the holy place" (v. 5, NKJV).

It seems incongruous to use the words "holy place" and "rubbish" in the same sentence. A holy place by its very nature should be clean. Hezekiah recognized this and therefore ordered that the trash be removed. Holiness and filthiness do not mix. They are incompatible. If that is true about a place, how much more it is true about the human heart. When God deals with the contamination of the human heart, He begins by removing the rubbish that has accumulated and making it clean. Only a clean heart is a fit dwelling place for the Holy Spirit.

Of course, it would be better to not let the rubbish accumulate in the first place. It is good to have a firm purpose to keep ourselves constantly unspotted by the world.

Question for Reflection: How long has it been since you emptied the "trash" from your life?

20

Qualification for Entry into God's Presence

> Who may ascend the hill of the LORD? Who may stand in his holy place? He who has clean hands and a pure heart, who does not lift up his soul to an idol or swear by what is false. —Ps. 24:3–4

Many people have a sense of inferiority about themselves. They constantly feel that they are not as good as other people—and not good enough for God. What about you? Are you "good enough" to enter God's presence? The good news is that we can be acceptable in God's sight. This psalm mentions four indications that we may enter God's presence.

The first is *clean hands*. Our hands represent what we do. God is primarily concerned with the moral content of our actions. Sinful actions bring guilt, which make our hands dirty. Only a thorough washing of stained hands can make them clean.

Next is *a pure heart*. Purity of heart involves a cleansing from a sinful nature. This is a ministry of the Holy Spirit, which is why He is symbolized by fire. Peter testified that this purification is what happened on the Day of Pentecost (Acts 15:9).

While the work of the Holy Spirit comes into a clearer focus in the New Testament, it is clearly recognized in the text that the problem of sin is twofold: committed sins resulting in guilt, and inherited depravity (the sinful nature). For that reason the complete solution is a two-step process: forgiveness and cleansing.

Third is *the absence of idolatry*. That means having absolute loyalty to God alone. God will not play second fiddle to lesser gods. Anything that takes the place that rightfully belongs to God becomes an idol.

Fourth is *sincerity and truth*. God will not tolerate falsehood. Those who worship Him must do it "in spirit and in truth." This requires honesty with God. He sees through our false pretenses. He cannot be fooled! He looks beyond outward appearances and sees what is in the heart.

It is a worthy goal to ascend the hill of the Lord and stand in His holy place. Are you ready?

Question for Reflection: What must you do to present yourself acceptably before God?

21

Cleansing

> Wash away all my iniquity and cleanse me from my sin. For I know my transgressions, and my sin is always before me.　　　　　—Ps. 51:2–3

What's the problem with people? It seems that everywhere you look there are signs that there is something gravely wrong with human beings. Just turn on any newscast and you'll see evidence that there is a fundamental problem with human nature. Uncontrolled hatred, greed, and violence cause incalculable pain and loss in our world every day. Across the millennia of human history you would think that we would learn, but in spite of all our efforts, the same old story keeps repeating itself. Why?

It is because the problem is located in the heart of human beings. To really change the world, the nature of a person must be changed on the inside. Only God can do that! He only does it when there is a sincere seeking for a pure heart. One of the key concepts of the holiness doctrine is that the solution of the sinful nature is the cleansing by the Holy Spirit. This truth is expressed by the psalmist in the text above in the form of a prayer. He recognized that something was wrong with him. He felt dirty on the inside. In desperation he looked up to God and pleaded, "Wash away all my iniquity and cleanse me from my sin." This was not a cry for a superficial job. The New King James Version preserves the urgency of the request with the words "wash me thoroughly."

Humankind has tried everything but God: education, law, money, medicine, reformation, drugs, war, bigger prisons, but none of these efforts have worked. It could even be argued that it keeps getting worse.

That is what makes heaven so attractive. Everyone there will have a cleansed heart, and all the consequences of sin will be banished forever.

Question for Reflection: Are you tired of trying to cleanse your own heart?

22

The Sinful Nature: How Did We Get It?

Surely I was sinful at birth, sinful from the time my mother conceived me.   —Ps. 51:5

Do you more closely resemble your father or your mother? Most of us have inherited at least a few of our characteristics from both parents. And there is one other trait you received as an inheritance from your spiritual ancestors: sin. We are all born with it.

After David recognized his sinful nature and sought cleansing, God gave him deeper insight into the problem. Just a couple of verses later, David discovers the source of the problem. He exclaims that he was already sinful at birth and that it originated when he was conceived. It was in the moment when he became identifiable as a human being.

After the fall of humankind, there was no way that unholy beings could transmit a holy nature to their offspring. Sin became part of human nature and was necessarily transmitted to the generations that followed. All human beings have it. It is most easily observed as "a bent toward sinning." It is the root from which all acts of sin become the fruit. We are sinners by nature even before we make the first choice to sin.

The work of reversing this condition is one of the ministries of the Holy Spirit, who is symbolized by fire. This became much more evident in the New Testament when we moved from the symbols and types of the Old Testament into the realities of the new covenant on the Day of Pentecost.

It is important to recognize that once the human heart has been cleansed, the person is no longer a sinner by nature and therefore incurs guilt when willful disobedience occurs. There are two ways to interpret the statement "I am a sinner saved by grace." One would be to say that while I was a sinner in the past, I have been saved by grace, which brought a wonderful change in my life so that I no longer willfully disobey God. A second interpretation would mean that although I continue to sin habitually, God overlooks that willful sin because of His grace. The first meaning is correct. The second is a contradiction. There is no place in Scripture that allows for persistent willful sinning. Repentance implies a sorrow for acts of sin that leads to quitting the practices.

Question for Reflection: Have you turned away from sin?

23

What a Contrast!

"Woe to me!" I cried. "I am ruined! For I am a man of unclean lips, and I live among a people of unclean lips, and my eyes have seen the King, the LORD Almighty."   —Isa. 6:5

Isaiah had an amazing, life-transforming experience. For a few moments God pulled back the curtain that separates this life from the next. Isaiah was overwhelmed by what he saw!

There was God sitting on His throne in all the splendor and glory of His holiness. What an impact it had! It was the contrast that was so startling. His vision of the holiness of God made his sinfulness stand out in stark contrast. His immediate cry was, "Woe to me! . . . I am ruined!" He had never noticed it before. It was seeing so clearly the holiness of God that made him so keenly aware of his own sinfulness.

When we compare ourselves to our neighbors or some other human being we may come out fairly well. But for a more accurate evaluation of our spiritual situation we will see it more clearly against the background of the holiness of God. Of course, it must be remembered that His holiness is absolute while ours is relative.

There is only one source of holiness. It does not exist apart from God. It does not consist of a commitment to a creed or submission to a list of rules. Holiness consists of a relationship with a person. It means being in harmony with the nature of God. If God is holy, and we relate to Him in such a way that there is no tension or conflict between us, then we share in the same nature. Holiness is the result of the removal of those things that are contrary to God. Such things are unholy. When they are gone only holiness remains. To be in harmony with God's nature is to be holy.

It would make a big difference if we could all see what Isaiah saw. After a vision of the glory of God's holiness, we could never be the same. For now, we'll have to take Isaiah's word for it. Once you have seen the reality, who would want to be anything but holy?

Question for Reflection: How does it make you feel when you contemplate the awesome nature of our God?

24

The Solution

> Then one of the seraphs flew to me with a live coal in his hand, which he had taken with tongs from the altar. With it he touched my mouth and said, "See, this has touched your lips; your guilt is taken away and your sin atoned for."   —Isa. 6:6–7

What solutions have you tried for cleansing your own nature of the stain of sin? People try all sorts of things—religious practices, meditation, asceticism. When Isaiah became painfully aware of his sinful condition, one of the seraphs knew just what he needed. Isaiah had symbolized his condition with the phrase "unclean lips." The seraph took a live coal from the altar and applied it at the point he perceived as being unclean. The body part is not what is important. We usually identify cleansing with the heart. It has nothing to do with the physical organ. It only symbolizes selfhood.

The important lesson here is simply how to deal with uncleanness: it must be purified. To use a red-hot coal certainly implies that it is not a superficial operation. Intense heat does an in-depth job. It brings to mind the process to which surgical instruments are submitted to make them fit for a major operation. They are subjected to heat and pressure in an autoclave for the amount of time required to kill even the most resistant germs.

Purity is the goal of God's operation on the human heart. Halfway measures will not suffice. It is clear in the Scripture that this purify-by-fire cleansing is the work of the Holy Spirit.

This is consistent with the New Testament imagery, which speaks of being baptized with the Holy Spirit and fire, the work of the Holy Spirit in the human heart that burns up the chaff, and the fire that appeared on the disciples on the Day of Pentecost.

The solutions to the sin problem that are attempted by

human beings do not work, but God knows just how to handle it. Burn it up! Get rid of it! Let the Holy Spirit do His work. Cleanse it away.

Question for Reflection: Will you allow the Holy Spirit to burn away the chaff from your life?

25

The Way of Holiness

And a highway will be there; it will be called the Way of Holiness. The unclean will not journey on it; it will be for those who walk in that Way; wicked fools will not go about on it.   —Isa. 35:8

Every road leads to a destination. So where you wind up will depend on which road you choose to take. This is even more important if the desired destination is heaven. The Bible calls it the Way of Holiness. It is the only road that will take us there.

There are two special requirements for those who walk on this highway. Nothing unclean is allowed to travel on this special way. It is reserved exclusively for those whose hearts have been cleansed. Neither will "wicked fools" be allowed to go about on it. In this world, fools surround us every day. People who trade lasting, eternal values for transient, worthless things are fools. People who deny the existence of God are fools. People who judge success in life by the accumulation of material things are fools. People who live for a few moments of illicit physical pleasure are fools. There are many different kinds of fools in the world. You will find them everywhere— except on the Way of Holiness.

Those who travel on the Way of Holiness are the ones who have discovered the true meaning of life. They are the ones who realize that what is at the end of this road makes it worthwhile at any cost. It is a glorious road.

Check your road map. Will the road you are on take you where you want to go? Watch out for detours. Don't get too close to the edge of the road. Keep moving ahead. Don't park somewhere to just enjoy the scenery. Enjoy the walk! Enjoy the fellowship with your fellow pilgrims. Be encouraged. You can make it. Heaven will be worth the effort.

Question for Reflection: Where is your life headed?

26

God's Holy People

They will be called the Holy People, the Redeemed of the LORD; and you will be called Sought After, the City No Longer Deserted. —Isa. 62:12

It is good to know that we are not alone in our quest for holiness. We are journeying together with many other people. God does not desire to merely create holy individuals. From the very beginning, God has been concerned about creating a race of holy people. In this text the prophet looks far into the future to catch a glimpse of the time when God's plan will become a reality. God's plan failed repeatedly as Israel turned away from Him to worship idols. But as Isaiah sees here, God's plan will eventually be accomplished in spite of the detours along the way.

It is a day we can all look forward to. What a privilege to be a part of God's holy people! He created us so He could enjoy us and we could enjoy Him. Then after we went astray, He redeemed us and restored us to a place of privilege and blessing.

Nothing less than a holy people could ever satisfy God. It is the basis of our fellowship and joy in His presence. It is because God is holy that He wants His people to be holy. Only God is holy by nature, but when we allow Him to do His sanctifying work in us we share the same nature. It leads to perfect harmony and unity in our relationship to Him. Simply stated, we share the same values and interests. We think alike with never a clash or disagreement.

God takes pleasure from His holy people and gives them special attention. He considers them a treasure. His redeemed will be called Sought After. It is amazing that sinful and unworthy though we were, He took the initiative and sought after us. They will also be called the City No Longer Deserted, which seems to point to God's faithfulness to His people. We can always count on His presence and blessing upon us.

Being a holy people not only puts us in harmony with God but also puts us in harmony with each other. Holiness requires us to love each other, share our burdens, and be mutually helpful on the journey.

Question for Reflection: Are you living and worshipping in harmony with God's people?

27

A New Covenant

"This is the covenant I will make with the house of Israel after that time," declares the LORD. "I will put my law in their minds and write it on their hearts. I will be their God, and they will be my people."
—Jer. 31:33

It has been said that nobody likes change, except for a wet baby. Perhaps one reason change is hard to accept is that it threatens the way we currently think or act. The greater the change, the more difficult it is to accept.

In one of the most important verses in the Old Testament, Jeremiah looked far into the future and foresaw some radical changes in the way God deals with humankind. God actually sounds disappointed that the old covenant was not working very well. It was based principally on outward forms of religion with little impact on ethical living. Nationalized religion was not producing individual responsibility. God let Jeremiah see some of the changes that would take place in the coming gospel age.

Under the new covenant the focus on religion would be internal rather than external. The laws previously written on tablets of stone will be written on human minds and hearts. The motivation to love and serve God will come from the inside rather than from external obligation. God will deal with internal principles rather than external symptoms.

With God's laws written on the heart, obedience to the Law will come from a desire to please God rather than a forced imposition under the threat of punishment. A moral transformation will take place by changing the heart.

With God's laws in our minds and hearts, it becomes our nature to obey them. They are not a grievous obligation imposed upon us. With a transformed nature we see God's laws in an entirely different light. We obey them because we want to, not out of fear, but because we love Him. We share the very nature from which the laws came in the first place.

Under the new covenant, there will be a new relationship to God, which will be less formal and more intimate, personal, spiritual, and individual. How fortunate we are to live in the age of the new covenant!

Question for Reflection: Do you have a personal relationship with God?

28

Pentecost Foreseen

I will sprinkle clean water on you, and you will be clean; I will cleanse you from all your impurities and from all your idols. I will give you a new heart and put

> a new spirit in you; I will remove from you your heart
> of stone and give you a heart of flesh. And I will put my
> Spirit in you and move you to follow my decrees and
> be careful to keep my laws. —Ezek. 36:25-27

Christians take for granted today things that seemed quite radical when they were first introduced. Ezekiel's words, which have been described as the high point of Old Testament prophecy, are like that. Ezekiel sees nothing less than the promise of heart purity, which received its fulfillment on the Day of Pentecost. Let's take a closer look.

"I will cleanse you": Peter testified that heart cleansing is what happened on the Day of Pentecost (Acts 15:9).

"A new heart": A new desire to love and serve God.

"A new spirit": A replacement of the spirit of rebellion and disobedience; an internal change of attitude.

"Remove from you your heart of stone": A hardened heart that stubbornly wants to go its own way.

"Give you a heart of flesh": A heart more sensitive and responsive to God.

"Put my Spirit within you": The indwelling of the Holy Spirit in His fullness. Note the capitalization of the word "Spirit." It is the dynamic of the Spirit that is the enabling power that makes it all possible.

In the New Testament age, this experience has become the norm of the Christian experience. Adam Clarke says, "Here is the salvation that is the birthright of every Christian believer; the complete destruction of sin in the soul, and the complete renewal of the heart; no sin having any place within, and no unrighteousness having any place without."

Question for Reflection: Is the Spirit of God living within you?

29

Filled with the Spirit

> And afterward, I will pour out my Spirit on all people. Your sons and daughters will prophesy, your old men will dream dreams, your young men will see visions. Even on my servants, both men and women, I will pour out my Spirit in those days.
> —Joel 2:28–29; see also Acts 2:16–21

Have you ever been impatient with God? It can be frustrating when He appears to take a long time to fulfill His promises. Imagine how the prophet Joel must have felt. He uttered this incredible prophecy hundreds of years before it was fulfilled. During his lifetime, Joel did not see this outpouring of the Holy Spirit, which came much later on the Day of Pentecost.

What a tremendous insight the prophet Joel had! It was an epochal event. Yes, the Spirit had come on certain individuals previously to enable them to do great exploits, but on this day He became available in a fuller measure to all people. This unprecedented outpouring of the Spirit inaugurated a new dispensation. It marked the birthday of the Church. The Holy Spirit became the Great Enabler, furnishing the power for the Church to accomplish its task in the world.

The experience of being "filled" with the Spirit elevated the human experience of God to its highest level. It is the most significant spiritual experience attainable in this world. The plan of redemption reached its climax when the door was opened for people to attain this level of intimacy with God's Spirit.

It took a long time to get ready for this event. A few of the prophets far in advance had glimpsed it on the horizon. But God is not in a hurry, and He always keeps His promises!

What a great privilege it is to live in the dispensation of the Holy Spirit. His fullness is available to all who seek Him today. Peter declared to the crowd of onlookers at Pentecost, "The promise is for you and your children and for all who are far off—for all whom the Lord our God will call" (Acts 2:39). It is not a special privilege reserved for a select few. It is for "all people."

Question for Reflection: Are you able to wait patiently for God's Spirit to work?

30

Purity Promised

> But who can endure the day of his coming? Who can stand when he appears? For he will be like a refiner's fire or a launderer's soap. He will sit as a refiner and purifier of silver; he will purify the Levites and refine them like gold and silver.　　　—Mal. 3:2–3

Some problems are not solved with quick fixes or easy answers. It often takes time and a good deal of effort to achieve a true solution. When we become impatient with God, we're not the first to do so. Others have found that His solutions are perfect—even though they may take some time.

Malachi had previously asked the question, "Where is the God of justice?" (2:17). To answer this question, he looks through the telescope of prophecy to identify events that will not transpire for several centuries. He sees the ministry of John the Baptist, the coming of the Messiah, the inauguration of a new covenant, the new method God will use to deal with sin, and the Final Judgment. He recognizes that no human being with a sinful nature could endure an encounter with a holy God. He implies that no one could stand in His presence, which is bad news. But now comes the good news!

God is going to deal with the problem of sin in a new and effective way. First, it will be like a refiner's fire. This metaphor is taken from the practice of purifying metal through a smelting process. The metal is heated into a molten state where the impurities rise to the top and are skimmed off. Second, it will be like a laundry process that uses a strong lye soap to bleach cloth and make it white. God's refining process is very effective. It removes the most stubborn stain and burns up the slightest impurity. He will purify the Levites (priests who were responsible for the degenerate state of Israel). In the new dispensation we are all priests, and therefore it applies to all of us.

What a wonderful glimpse the prophet had of the wonderful solution God would offer for humankind's biggest problem! It is not a superficial Band-Aid type of treatment. It goes to the core of the problem and deals with it in a radical way that destroys the evil and results in purity of heart. This enables us to offer ourselves to God in righteousness and holiness.

Question for Reflection: Are you looking for a quick fix to the problem of sin?

Holiness in the New Testament

After centuries of waiting and anticipating, the time had come. Jesus had been sent on His mission to earth; it was time for a giant leap forward in the revelation of God's plan of redemption. One of the first indications was the announcement by John the Baptist that a new baptism—with fire—was soon coming. It happened on the Day of Pentecost, when the Holy Spirit came upon the disciples, purified their hearts, and filled them with His presence in a measure they had never experienced before. This became the New Testament standard for Christian experience.

All of the types, symbols, rituals, ceremonies, and shadows had become a glorious reality. Real holiness was now obtainable through consecration and the cleansing act of the Holy Spirit. The New Testament writers would now approach it as an accomplished fact rather than a future hope. The Church was born. The Holy Spirit became its dynamic (its moving force), which made it complete and equipped it for its mission. Previously there had been occasions when the Holy Spirit had come upon certain individuals to empower them for a specific task, but now His presence and power were available to all believers.

Everything is different now. It is a new dispensation. Real holiness of heart is attainable. Real power is available. The Comforter has come!

31

Baptism with the Holy Spirit and Fire

I baptize you with water for repentance. But after me will come one who is more powerful than I, whose sandals I am not fit to carry. He will baptize you with the Holy Spirit and fire. His winnowing fork is in his hand, and He will clear his threshing floor, gathering the wheat into the barn and burning up the chaff with unquenchable fire. —Matt. 3:11–12

The time had finally arrived. After many centuries of revelation and preparation, the Messiah had come to earth. True, it happened differently than most expected. He was lying in a manger in a stable behind the inn in the unpretentious town of Bethlehem.

That night would later be recognized as the dividing point of all time, separating all that had taken place previously from all that would follow. From that point everything would be different. Until that time, much of God's revelation was contained in shadows, types, ceremonies, ritual, and symbols. Now, through the teaching of the Son of God in person, radical truth would shine forth as blazing light. No one had ever spoken like Him with such authority and power.

It is not surprising that some of the big changes that would take place would be announced by the designated precursor of Christ who was sent to prepare the way for Him. John the Baptist had insight into one of the most significant events that would take place in the new dispensation. His prophecy is recorded in the third chapter of the New Testament: the baptism with the Holy Spirit and fire.

This baptism with the Holy Spirit would bring more intimacy with God and the manifestation of greater power in the lives of believers. The baptism with fire would destroy the carnal nature and bring purity of heart in a way not previously possible. This experience would mark the beginning of a new era in God's redemptive plan.

Question for Reflection: Are you ready for God to do something new in your life?

32

Prelude to Being Filled with the Holy Spirit

Blessed are those who hunger and thirst for righteousness, for they will be filled.　　　—Matt. 5:6

Have you ever had a craving—a desire for something that seemed overwhelming and insatiable? Most often, we hunger or thirst for our favorite type of food or beverage. Can you imagine having that kind of deep hunger filled with holiness?

In what has been called the Sermon on the Mount, Jesus is setting forth the principles of His kingdom. In one simple sentence He opens the possibility of being filled with righteousness (or holiness), and the condition that is required to make it happen.

This wonderful grace is not given to those who seek it halfheartedly. It must be sought with an intense desire. In fact, the seeker must come to the place where he or she wants it more than anything else! The picture presented here is the desire of a person who is starving for food or the person lost in a desert who is about to perish for lack of a drink of water. In both of these cases the desire is so overwhelming that anyone would pay most any price for it.

It reminds me of a story that reveals the real important things of life. A man was crossing the desert and was near the point of perishing for lack of water. Suddenly he spied a canteen lying on the sand in the distance. Thinking that it must have fallen from a passing caravan, he desperately ran to retrieve it. When he picked it up and opened it, his anguished cry was, "Oh no! It is only filled with pearls." It had no value because it didn't meet his desperate need.

How badly do you want to be delivered from the sinful nature that robs you of spiritual victory? Do you long to be filled with the Holy Spirit? Would you be willing to pay any price for it? Well, it is available to those who seek it with their whole heart. It will be denied to those who only have a casual interest.

The price is high, but it is a great bargain!

Question for Reflection: What is your greatest hunger?

33

Who Will See God?

Blessed are the pure in heart, for they will see God.
—Matt. 5:8

One of the most beautiful things about the Beatitudes is their simplicity. Here, in the preamble to the Sermon on the Mount, Jesus expresses the principles of the Christian life in clear, unmistakable language. These matters are far too important to risk confusion, and the Master goes right to the heart of the matter. Surely the most important question for any human being is to discover the requirement for a person to see God. We understand this to mean to enter into His heavenly abode and live with Him forever. What could be more important than that?

What does God require to receive such a wonderful gift? You would think that something so priceless would be difficult to achieve. It is not knowledge, or intelligence, or great accomplishments, or sacrifice. There is only one key that will unlock the door to heaven: a pure heart.

The good part is that all of the resources needed to attain a pure heart have already been provided. This does not mean that it is cheap. It requires a profound and complete consecration of all that you have and are. It means putting God at the center of your life and letting Him take control. It means loving God more than anything else. It means giving Him permission to cleanse you from your sinful nature and putting Him in control of your life. It means coming into perfect harmony with God. It means full salvation from sin in all of its forms.

Unless you allow Him to cleanse your heart, you have no other scriptural hope of ever being with Him. Peter clearly identified this purity of heart as the essence of the work of the Holy Spirit on the Day of Pentecost (see Acts 15:9).

Question for Reflection: What is the condition of your heart?

34

Christian Perfection

Be perfect, therefore, as your heavenly Father is perfect.   —Matt. 5:48

How often we have heard it said, "Nobody's perfect!" Most of us would probably agree with that statement if we did not give it too much thought. However, the word "perfect" is undeniably a scriptural term, and Jesus here makes the amazing statement that some kind of perfection is possible for believers. What does He mean?

Obviously, it does not mean absolute perfection, for that pertains only to God. However, there are certain spiritual areas where a relative perfection is attainable to us.

For example, the Bible makes it clear that it is possible to live without sinning. All committed sin is the result of a choice, and the Bible promises that we will never be tempted beyond what we can bear. No one can ever truthfully say, "I had to sin. There was no other way out!" There is no power on earth that can make you choose to disobey God if you purpose in your heart not to do it. You can make a mistake, but that is different from a deliberate choice to disobey God. Mistakes have good intentions.

Love can also be perfected. The Bible commands us to love God with our whole heart, soul, mind, and strength. Would that not be perfect love? What could be missing?

Would God command it if it were impossible? God is only satisfied with genuine love that is not flawed. My guess is that you also want that kind of love from your spouse!

Then there is perfection of motive or intention. It is true that our actions may not always turn out well, but our intentions can always be good.

God has set the standard of our relationship with Him to be of the very highest quality. If we have sincerely done our best to love and serve Him, He will be satisfied with that. If He sets a standard for us, He will make it possible to attain it.

Question for Reflection: Are you striving for perfection?

35

A Prayer for Holiness

Your kingdom come, your will be done on earth as it is in heaven.   —Matt. 6:10

What do you usually pray about? We seem to pray most often about our most immediate needs or problems. We pray for healing, financial help, or guidance in dealing with difficult people or situations. But have you ever thought to pray about the things that are of greatest concern to God?

The disciples came to Jesus and asked Him to teach them to pray. They had no doubt noticed how important prayer was to Him. He responded by giving them a brief example of a model prayer. The first petition in it was the text above, a plea for His kingdom to come and His will to be done.

Those words cannot be sincerely repeated without seeking for holiness. If you want His will to be done, you must start with your own heart and life. It would be an insincere and invalid prayer for you to ask for His will to be done in every situation but your own.

Do you want God's will to be done in your life? Then you

must seek sanctification, for the Bible clearly states that "it is God's will that you should be sanctified" (1 Thess. 4:3).

If you want God's will to be done, you may need to adjust your own will so that it is not in conflict with His. Even Jesus had to do this when He prayed, "Yet not as I will, but as you will" (Matt. 26:39).

The point is that this kind of praying leads to entire sanctification. Consecration is the requirement, and it takes place in the moment that you surrender to God and bring your will into submission with His.

There can be no doubt that God's will is being done and His kingdom has come in heaven. It is for that reason that it is such a wonderful place. However, it is possible to have a little bit of heaven right here on earth. It is always a wonderful thing to be where God's will is being done. That can happen in the depths of your being, when the Holy Spirit cleanses you from your sinful nature and He molds you into Christ's likeness.

Question for Reflection: Have you prayed for your own sanctification?

36

Holiness Simplified

Love the Lord your God with all your heart and with all your soul and with all your mind and with all your strength.   —Mark 12:30

In a marriage relationship, there is such a thing as obligation. We take wedding vows that promise to be faithful, come what may. Yet duty is not what forms the true bond in marriage—it is love. The same is true of our relationship with God. We do not obey Him because we have to but because we want to love Him. So in its simplest form, holiness can be described as loving God with all of your heart.

The requirement for entire sanctification is a complete consecration to God. But consecration is not the price we pay to escape hell. Neither is it a penalty we must pay in order to please God and receive His blessing upon us. It is not something we do because a harsh tyrant demands it. Consecration is an act of love! The more we love God, the more we want to be consecrated to Him. We want to seek His will because we know it is the best for us. He wants to bless us and do good things for us.

So as we grow in our love for Him, our consecration may be progressive. But if our love keeps growing, we will eventually get to the place where we will meet the standard outlined in our text above. At that point it can be said that we love God more than anything else. We have then met the requirement for entire sanctification! The bottom-line essence of entire sanctification is nothing more or less than loving God completely.

For example, if you love God with this kind of love, you will want to serve Him and please Him in all that you do. You will seek His will in all things. Total love will compel you to do it. Doing God's will and pleasing Him will be your top priority.

On the other hand, if your love for God has been perfected, you could not even think of disobeying Him or doing anything that would be displeasing to Him. Your complete love for Him motivates you to never enter into conflict with Him.

Your love is what God wants more than anything else. It really simplifies the whole process to think of holiness as getting to the place where you love God as He wants you to love Him.

Question for Reflection: How deep is your love for God?

37

The Enabling Power of God

To rescue us from the hand of our enemies, and to enable us to serve him without fear in holiness and righteousness before him all our days.

—Luke 1:74–75

What are the things in life that you will never accomplish? Most of us realize that there are a few achievements that are probably beyond our reach. You may be resigned to the fact that you will not climb Mount Everest or play at Carnegie Hall or become president of your country. It's not that we lack ambition; we simply know our limits.

Is holiness on that list of things that you think you can't do?

This prophecy is a part of the Song of Zechariah, which was part of the celebration of the birth of John the Baptist. It is based on the covenant God made under oath to Abraham. Notice the six elements within it.

1. The triumph over our enemies. Satan is our worst enemy, but we are assured that righteousness will triumph over evil in the end.

2. We have this assurance because of a covenant God made under oath, which guarantees it will happen. God keeps His promises!

3. In spite of our human weaknesses, God will enable us to achieve this significant victory. It will be won by the power of God working in us.

4. This great victory consists of the power to serve God without fear (the fear of defeat or failure).

5. The glorious possibility of living in holiness and righteousness. Here is where we reach the highest potential of God's grace.

6. Note that this is not a temporary or sporadic condition. It is specifically defined as a condition, which applies to "all

our days." To serve the Lord full time, all our days, in holiness, should be the goal of every Christian.

The task may seem daunting at times, but remember, it doesn't depend on you. God enables us to do all He asks of us. When the Holy Spirit comes to fill us and take control, His power is at work within us. As Paul said, "I can do all things through Christ who strengthens me" (Phil. 4:13, NKJV). When you are tempted to say, "I can't," just remember that He can! With God nothing is impossible.

Question for Reflection: Do you believe it is possible for you to become holy?

38

The Best Gift

> If you then, though you are evil, know how to give good gifts to your children, how much more will your Father in heaven give the Holy Spirit to those who ask him! —Luke 11:13

Good fathers like to give good gifts to their children. That is simply because they love them. Love is a powerful motivator. On any gift-giving occasion we can imagine a loving father searching for the best possible gift he can give for the benefit of his child.

The message of this text is that if it is true on the human level, how much more it is true of our Heavenly Father. God loves His children and always wants to give them His best. If that is true, which it is, we might ask, what is the best gift God could give to one of His children? Now, stretch your imagination! What would be the ultimate gift to be given by Almighty God, who can do whatever He wants with no limitations? Would it be wealth or material things? Evidently not! He has chosen to give His Holy Spirit to those He loves. It is hard to even comprehend the value of this gift. It cannot be calculated in human terms. Think of it as the living, indwelling Spirit of God in a most intimate relationship constantly on call to comfort, guide, and empower for any need that may arise. How incredible is the goodness of God!

And better yet, He is not given arbitrarily. God gives the Holy Spirit to "those who ask him." Our loss is great because we lack the faith to ask for God's promises.

The only catch is that our hearts must be prepared to receive what He wants to give us. The Holy Spirit cannot take up His abode in a "home" that is contaminated by sin. He must be given permission to "clean the house" before He moves in. This He willingly does for both our benefit and His.

Question for Reflection: What have you been asking God for?

39

Better Without Jesus?

But I tell you the truth: It is for your good that I am going away. Unless I go away, the Counselor will not come to you; but if I go, I will send him to you.

—John 16:7

The empty nest can be a difficult time for both parents and children. Children may fear that they cannot adequately make their own way in the world, and parents sometimes feel the loss of their children's presence. But growing up is both inevitable and good. God designed us to move from one life stage to another. Jesus designed His relationship with the disciples in the same way. He intended for them to move from being dependent on Him to being guided by the Holy Spirit.

These words of Jesus must have been confusing to the disciples. Jesus had just announced that He was leaving them and then added that it was better that way. They must have been thinking, "Are you kidding? How can that be?" They had come to depend on Him. He was the One who had trained them and given them the guidance they desperately needed. What would they do without Him?

Then Jesus went on to explain that something new, different, and very significant was about to happen. The Holy Spirit (the Counselor) would soon come to inaugurate His special ministry in the world. Even though it was hard to understand at the moment, it would be an improvement! Why was Jesus' departure a good thing?

While Jesus was physically in the world, His sphere of influence was limited to a rather small geographical location. He had contact with only relatively few persons in Palestine. In contrast the Holy Spirit would minister to the entire human race simultaneously.

We can think of the Father as the Originator of the great plan of salvation. Jesus was the Provider who made it possible by His work on the Cross. The Holy Spirit is the Executor who takes the plan and the provisions and applies them to individual hearts and lives. His work is done on the inside. (See John 14:17.) He is the One who initiates salvation by convicting us of our sin and guilt. He is the One who carries out the infusion of spiritual life in the new birth. He is the One who cleanses the heart from the sinful nature through a baptism. He is the One who "comes alongside" us in our journey to meet our needs by giving comfort, guidance, and strength. Truly, it was good for Jesus to go back to heaven so He could send the Holy Spirit.

Question for Reflection: Have you developed a relationship with the Holy Spirit?

40

When Jesus Prayed for Me

My prayer is not that you take them out of the world but that you protect them from the evil one. They are not of the world, even as I am not of it. Sanctify them by the truth; your word is truth. As you sent me into the world, I have sent them into the world. For them I sanctify myself, that they too may be truly sanctified. —John 17:15–19

Parents often want better things for their children than the children want for themselves. Parents want their kids to succeed in life, to be healthy, and to love the Lord. Usually, kids just want to have fun! It should be no surprise that God wants something more for us than we have set our sights on—He wants us to be holy.

On the night before He was crucified, Jesus prayed this prayer for His disciples. It is one of the "holy of holies" of the New Testament. From this prayer, we get deep insight into the things He was most concerned about regarding His disciples. He prayed for their protection and their unity. But, the very heart of His prayer was the request that they be sanctified. In the Old Testament the word "sanctify" was used to "set apart" things for sacred purposes. But in the New Testament it refers to the work of the Holy Spirit to purify the heart of a person and make it holy. This prayer of Jesus for His disciples was answered on the Day of Pentecost. Peter later identified that day as the moment when their hearts were purified. (See Acts 15:9.)

What a difference it made in the lives of the disciples! Before Pentecost they were arguing about who would have the most prominent place in the coming Kingdom. All of them fled in fear when the authorities came to arrest Jesus. Three times Peter flatly denied that he even knew Him. But after Pentecost they were bold and fearless and willing to lay down their lives. They had a power they did not have previously. That is why Jesus told them not to respond to the Great Commission He had just given them but rather to wait in Jerusalem for the "promise of the Father," which would equip them for the task ahead. There would be no more evidence of selfish ambition or personal pride.

Jesus stated that He sanctified himself (set himself apart) so that the disciples could be "truly sanctified" (purified and made holy).

How important it is today for all of us to experience our personal Pentecost! The future of the Church depends on it.

Question for Reflection: Are you seeking God's best for yourself?

41

The Promise of Power

But you will receive power when the Holy Spirit comes on you; and you will be my witnesses in Jerusalem, and in all Judea and Samaria, and to the ends of the earth.   —Acts 1:8

One of the key ingredients for success in any endeavor is to have the right resources. A business can't succeed without capital, and an employee can't perform well without tools or equipment. Likewise, we won't be successful in our quest for holiness without this key factor—the Holy Spirit.

Jesus knew very well that if the disciples tried to carry out their mission to the world in human power they would not get very far. There was something more they still needed. He had given them some hints about it, but it had not yet happened. However, it had been promised by the Father. The disciples must have wondered what it was that had been promised.

However, they did take the words of Jesus seriously. They

went to Jerusalem and started a prayer meeting that lasted for 10 days. Since they really didn't know what they were expecting, it is commendable that they waited that long. Jesus must have impressed them of its importance.

They had just three clues: (1) It had to do with a special baptism. (2) They were going to receive power from it. (3) With that power, they would be witnesses to the ends of the earth.

The power that they were to receive was not a separate package. It would come from a new relationship with the Holy Spirit. He would fill them in a measure they had not had previously. He would move from being "with" them to being "in" them. (See John 14:17.) His presence would be the source of their power.

It is important to notice the purpose of this power. It was not to be used for prestige or personal aggrandizement. It was not for the purpose of calling attention to themselves or gaining recognition. It was strictly for enabling them to do the work God had called them to do.

History tells the rest of the story. They went out with an aggressive spirit of evangelism that impacted the world. (All of them except one became martyrs.) We still need that same power to be effective in our world.

Question for Reflection: Are you seeking the Holy Spirit?

42

It Finally Happened!

When the day of Pentecost came, they were all together in one place. Suddenly a sound like the blowing of a violent wind came from heaven and filled the whole house where they were sitting. They saw what seemed to be tongues of fire that separated and came to rest on each of them. All of them were filled with the Holy Spirit and began to speak in other tongues as the Spirit enabled them.

—Acts 2:1–4

Some important events pass by quietly, almost unnoticed, while others arrive with great fanfare. When the Holy Spirit descended on the disciples on the Day of Pentecost, there was no mistaking the occasion—God was in the house!

An outpouring of the Holy Spirit had been prophesied and anticipated for centuries. It was clear that it would be an epochal event with a tremendous impact on the Church and the world. The scriptures above relate the story of the moment when it actually happened.

Since it was the inauguration of a new era in history, it was accompanied by signs and symbols that helped clarify what was taking place.

1. The "sound like the blowing of a violent wind." Maybe it was like a tornado! This was to alert them to the importance of what was about to happen. It could also be thought of as a symbol of the power they were going to receive.

2. The "tongues of fire" that came to rest on each of them. Fire is recognized as a purifying agent and fulfilled the prophecy that it would be a baptism with fire.

3. "All of them were filled with the Holy Spirit." This is the essence of the Pentecostal experience. The other signs were temporary and peripheral. The filling with the Holy Spirit was the main event!

4. ". . . and began to speak in other tongues as the Spirit enabled them." This was a miracle of communication. The writer goes out of his way to offer proofs that these were real languages. They were given specifically to communicate the message of Pentecost to the observers. It is additional proof that the message was for all nations.

Question for Reflection: What is the sign of the Spirit's presence in your life?

43

Pentecost: Not an Afterthought

No, this is what was spoken by the prophet Joel: "In the last days, God says, I will pour out my Spirit on all people. Your sons and daughters will prophesy, your young men will see visions, your old men will dream dreams. Even on my servants, both men and women, I will pour out my Spirit in those days, and they will prophesy."   —Acts 2:16–18

There is nothing new about the Holy Spirit. The third person of the Trinity has been active throughout recorded history. The Spirit's presence at Pentecost did not pop up unexpectedly. It was the culmination of God's plan that had been anticipated for many centuries. Several of the prophets, such as Jeremiah, Ezekiel, and Joel, had foreseen the outpouring of the Holy Spirit more than eight hundred years before it happened.

There are numerous cases in the Old Testament when the Spirit came upon key individuals, enabling them to perform heroic exploits for a specific purpose. However, this is not to be confused with the new dispensation in the New Testament where the Holy Spirit became available to all believers who seek His fullness. This experience became the norm for all Christians after Pentecost.

The fullness of the Spirit should be thought of as the maximum work of God in the human heart. There is nothing in God's marvelous plan that is better than this! Everything that had happened since Genesis was in preparation for this day. Since Pentecost, we believers have privileges and blessings unknown to human beings before. They include new power, a greater intimacy and fellowship with God, and the cleansing of the sinful nature leading to complete victory over sin.

God had planned it this way from the beginning. The revelation of His plan was progressive throughout history. But it was only after Jesus came that the final stages of the plan became complete.

It is a special privilege to live in the dispensation of the Holy Spirit, and to enjoy all the blessings of His ministry.

Question for Reflection: Are you living in the Spirit?

44

Pentecost Repeated

> After they prayed, the place where they were meeting was shaken. And they were all filled with the Holy Spirit and spoke the word of God boldly.
>
> —Acts 4:31

Every time a sports team wins a championship, there is speculation about whether or not it can repeat the feat. Most don't, of course. Such incredible achievements are often a once-in-a-lifetime event.

That's not true of the Day of Pentecost. The baptism with the Holy Spirit was not a one-time experience intended only for a special, elite group. Peter emphatically denied that that was the case in his public message on the same day it happened: "The promise is for you and your children and for all who are far off—for all whom the Lord our God will call" (2:39). Also, the baptism was repeated on several occasions.

Peter and John had just had a run-in with the Sanhedrin. They had been jailed. When they were later released, "They went back to their own people and reported" (4:23). Obviously not all believers had been present with the 120 in the Upper Room. After hearing the powerful report from Peter, the power of God came upon them and Pentecost was repeated for their benefit.

When the apostles heard that there had been a revival in Samaria under the preaching of Philip, they sent Peter and

John there to follow up. "When they arrived, they prayed for them that they might receive the Holy Spirit, because the Holy Spirit had not yet come upon any of them; they had simply been baptized into the name of the Lord Jesus. Then Peter and John placed their hands on them, and they received the Holy Spirit" (8:15–17).

Philip's evangelistic campaign had great success as many "accepted the word of God" (v. 14). Peter and John had specifically gone there to introduce them to the deeper work of the Holy Spirit. Once again Pentecost was repeated. This is a classic example of two works of grace: conversion and subsequently the filling with the Holy Spirit.

Pentecost has continued to be repeated across the centuries. Thousands upon thousands of believers have given testimony to it.

Question for Reflection: Have you been baptized with the Spirit?

45

A Chosen Instrument

But the Lord said to Ananias, "Go! This man is my chosen instrument to carry my name before the Gentiles and their kings and before the people of Israel. I will show him how much he must suffer for my name." Then Ananias went to the house and entered it. Placing his hands on Saul, he said, "Brother Saul, the Lord—Jesus, who appeared to you on the road as you were coming here—has sent me so that you may see again and be filled with the Holy Spirit."   —Acts 9:15–17

God often uses the most unlikely people to fulfill His purposes. That was true of Gideon, for example, the unlikely hero who led God's people to a great victory. It was also true of Saul, whom we know as Paul—the persecutor of Christians who became the greatest of all evangelists.

Paul was on his way to Damascus for the specific purpose of persecuting the Christians there. But God had other plans for him. God could see in this man the characteristics of his personality and the abilities that could make him a mighty instrument to impact the world for the kingdom of God. So God arranged to have an encounter with him along the road that day.

When Jesus himself confronted him, he was blinded. He immediately realized how wrong he had been and humbly inquired what Jesus wanted him to do. He was instructed to proceed into Damascus and wait. It cannot be doubted that Paul experienced a dramatic conversion at that moment.

There was something more he needed, however, if he was to become a powerful instrument to be used of God. God chose another one of His servants, Ananias, to take the message to him. While reluctant at first, Ananias did comply with his mission. His words to Paul were (above) that God had sent him so he would receive his sight and be filled with the Holy Spirit.

Subsequent history proved the validity of that experience. God used him perhaps more than any other person in history to extend the Kingdom and to take the gospel to the Gentiles.

The possibility is still open today as to what God can do with a person totally surrendered to Him and empowered by His Spirit.

Question for Reflection: Do you think God can use you?

46

The Gentile Pentecost

While Peter was still speaking these words, the Holy Spirit came on all who heard the message. The circumcised believers who had come with Peter were astonished that the gift of the Holy Spirit had been poured out even on the Gentiles.   —Acts 10:44–45

God's plan is huge—it encompasses everyone. It may be tempting to think that God's grace is reserved for a few special people, but God loves everyone and is eager to see others saved and cleansed from sin.

That is what we learn from the story of Cornelius, a Roman army officer who had become a devout Christian. He was also a Gentile (not Jewish). God had told him to send for Peter who would have a special message for him. In the meantime, God was dealing with Peter in a special way to get him ready for the encounter. He was a guest in a home about 80 miles away. While he was praying on the rooftop, he had a vision of all kinds of animals let down from heaven in a sheet. He was instructed to "kill and eat." Peter objected, "I have never eaten anything impure or unclean." The response was, "Do not call anything impure that God has made clean" (9:13-15).

Peter was wondering about the meaning of this vision when the men from Caesarea arrived at the front gate and called for him. He left with them the next day for the house of Cornelius. When they arrived, Peter discovered that Cornelius had assembled "a large gathering" (10:27) of his relatives and friends to hear him.

While Peter was still speaking, "the Holy Spirit came on all who heard the message" (v. 44). Astonished, Peter exclaimed, "They have received the Holy Spirit just as we have" (v. 47). The amazing thing was not only that Pentecost had been repeated again but also that these were Gentiles! This was completely contrary to all that the Jews believed about their exclusive special relationship to God. Yet it was undeniable.

This fact had a revolutionary effect on the entire remaining history of the Church. Our God is the God of all nations and bestows His gifts impartially on all people who meet the conditions to receive them.

Question for Reflection: Is there someone in your life who needs to hear about God's redeeming love?

47

The Opposition Begins

> As I began to speak, the Holy Spirit came on them as he had come on us at the beginning. Then I remembered what the Lord had said: "John baptized with water, but you will be baptized with the Holy Spirit." So if God gave them the same gift as he gave us, who believed in the Lord Jesus Christ, who was I to think that I could oppose God! —Acts 11:15–17

God has a way of taking people out of their comfort zones. We would usually rather stay where we are, safe and comfortable, than to allow new and different experiences in our lives. But to stay where we are is to miss God's best for us.

After Peter's experience at Joppa and Caesarea, the word spread rapidly about what had happened. When the news reached Jerusalem, some of the Jews were horrified by what they heard. When Peter arrived back in Jerusalem, a confrontation was inevitable. The accusation was that he had gone into the house of uncircumcised men and eaten with them. This was a serious breach of Jewish law and tradition.

Peter wisely began his defense by relating the entire story in detail: his experience in Joppa, the trip to Caesarea, and the descent of the Holy Spirit. His defense essentially was that he did not give them the Holy Spirit: God did! He just happened to be there when it happened. After all, who are we to oppose what God does? It was an unanswerable argument. The crisis was averted.

The next challenge came from Antioch. Some of the troublemakers began to teach that people could not be saved without circumcision. Paul and Barnabas strongly opposed this teaching. It became obvious that this issue needed to be solved once and for all in an official manner. So they sent Paul and Barnabas to Jerusalem to consult with the apostles and elders and reach a decision. When they met, there was much discussion, including speeches by Peter, Paul, and Barnabas. The conclusion was finally reached that since salvation was by grace, conforming to Jewish tradition could not be required. The argument was: "God, who knows the heart, showed that he accepted them by giving the Holy Spirit to them, just as he did to us. He made no distinction between us and them, for he purified their hearts by faith" (15:8–9).

Question for Reflection: Are you ready to experience whatever God has in store for you?

48

An Error Corrected

Meanwhile a Jew named Apollos, a native of Alexandria, came to Ephesus. He was a learned man, with a thorough knowledge of the Scriptures. He had been instructed in the way of the Lord, and he spoke with great fervor and taught about Jesus accurately, though he knew only the baptism of John. He began to speak boldly in the synagogue. When Priscilla and Aquila heard him, they invited him to their home and explained to him the way of God more adequately.

—Acts 18:24–26

Knowledge is one thing; experience is something else

altogether. Anyone who has studied geography in grade school can locate the Grand Canyon on a map. Those who have stood at its rim, however, and felt the incredible dry heat and seen the breathtaking grandeur of this wonder of the world truly understand how magnificent it is. Experience surpasses knowledge every time.

So while Apollos is described as a "learned man" who "spoke with great fervor" and "taught about Jesus accurately," he lacked the experience of the fullness of God's Holy Spirit. He knew only the baptism of John. Priscilla and Aquila recognized the limitation of his knowledge and "explained to him the way of God more adequately." His teaching about Jesus was good as far as it went, but fell short, because he did not know about another baptism of the Spirit.

Unfortunately, there are many Christians in the church today who are in a similar situation. They may have truly experienced the baptism of repentance, but have not moved forward to the baptism of the Spirit. In some cases it may be due to the fact that they have teachers like Apollos who know "only the baptism of John."

In other cases, a person's experience may go beyond the theology they have been taught. It is possible to be a Spirit-filled Christian without knowing what to call it. It is not uncommon for a person to hear the preaching of holiness and to exclaim, "Yes, that's exactly what I experienced several years ago." It is important that preachers and teachers experience the fullness of the Spirit themselves so they can testify to it and instruct others properly.

Fortunately, Apollos came into contact with more mature Christians who were able to explain some things to him "more adequately." They didn't do it in an embarrassing way, but rather invited him to their home where they could converse with him in private.

We could certainly use more Priscillas and Aquilas today.

Question for Reflection: Have you had an experience of God's Spirit?

49

An Important Discovery

While Apollos was at Corinth, Paul took the road through the interior and arrived at Ephesus. There he found some disciples and asked them, "Did you receive the Holy Spirit when you believed?" They answered, "No, we have not even heard that there is a Holy Spirit." . . . When Paul placed his hands on them, the Holy Spirit came on them, and they spoke in tongues and prophesied.   —Acts 19:1–2, 6

Have you ever felt that you were missing something? Perhaps you left the house one morning and had the nagging feeling that you had left some important papers behind. Or maybe you've entered a conversation late only to realize that you had no idea what was being discussed. When Paul came to Ephesus, he came into contact with a group of 12 believers who were having a similar experience. They were missing something vitally important in their spiritual lives. Paul asked them if they had received the Holy Spirit. They replied that they did not even know that there was a Holy Spirit! It did not take Paul long to remedy the situation. Before their meeting was over they were all filled with the Holy Spirit.

This text clearly teaches that entire sanctification is a second work of grace. These 12 men were clearly identified as disciples of Christ, but until Paul asked the question, they were not even aware of the existence of the Holy Spirit.

Paul's example shows us that as Christian leaders, we need to ask the same question to those who need to be guided into the deeper experiences of the Holy Spirit.

This is very important because one of the principal reasons why new Christians may fall away from their newfound faith is because they are not encouraged to move ahead and seek the deeper experiences of the Holy Spirit. It is one of the key factors that bring strength and stability to the Christian life. Those who do not move ahead quickly on the highway of holiness are much more likely to go backward. It is much like an airplane: When it stops moving forward, it starts to go down.

Holiness is not just a spiritual luxury that is optional. It is truly indispensable to a victorious Christian life. Neither is it like a dessert offered after the main meal that can be enjoyed or declined at the discretion of the diner. We really need the Holy Spirit!

Question for Reflection: Is there something missing from your spiritual life?

50

The Inheritance of the Sanctified

Now I commit you to God and to the word of his grace, which can build you up and give you an inheritance among all those who are sanctified.
—Acts 20:32; see also Acts 26:18

Every year, thousands of dollars go unclaimed because those who should inherit them have no idea that they have a legacy coming to them. Their benefactors, usually distant relatives, die without leaving a will. The next of kin, who should inherit their estate, cannot be located and so miss out on the prize.

There is a special inheritance promised to all who are sanctified, yet it often goes unclaimed. Some other scriptures give us a clue as to the nature of this inheritance: "Now if we are children, then we are heirs—heirs of God and co-heirs with Christ, if indeed we share in his sufferings in order that we may also share in his glory" (Rom. 8:17). Our inheritance is based on our relationship to God as sons and daughters. Jesus was also a Son of God, which makes us coheirs with Him.

- The inheritance is described as a kingdom (Matt. 25:34).
- It is described as "glorious" (Eph 1:18).

- It is said to be kept for us in heaven and will never "perish, spoil or fade" (1 Pet. 1:4).
- It is eternal in duration, meaning it will last forever (Heb. 9:15).
- It will be delivered to us on the Day of Judgment (Matt. 25:34).

What an inheritance! There is still a lot that remains to be revealed about it, but we can affirm with certainty that it will be worth any sacrifice to qualify for it.

A person may be poor in terms of this world's goods, and at the same time rich considering the promised inheritance. It is a sure thing—just a matter of time!

Do not overlook the fact that it is only promised to all those who are sanctified. That means to all who are fully committed to God, whose hearts are pure and holy.

The knowledge of this promise ought to be encouraging to the pilgrims on the highway of holiness, especially during difficult times, even when carrying a heavy burden.

Question for Reflection: Are you looking forward to the prize?

51

Circumcision of the Heart

A man is not a Jew if he is only one outwardly, nor is circumcision merely outward and physical. No, a man is a Jew if he is one inwardly; and circumcision is circumcision of the heart, by the Spirit, not by the written code. Such a man's praise is not from men, but from God.   —Rom. 2:28–29

Which is more important, to wear your wedding ring every day or to be faithful to your spouse? Obviously, it is more important to be faithful. The ring is merely a symbol of the marriage commitment—without fidelity, the ring means nothing.

Circumcision, the symbol that God had ordained as a sign of His special relationship with the Jews, was meant to identify them as God's chosen people. However, with the passing of time, the practice came to lose its meaning. In the New Testament, some of the Jews argued that a person could not be saved without being circumcised. This caused considerable discussion in the Early Church inasmuch as God had made it clear that salvation was also available to the Gentiles.

Paul argued that physical circumcision was of no value at all. It was keeping the commands that really counted (1 Cor. 7:18). He saw that defining a person's relationship to God by a physical sign could have the effect of making Christ of no value (Gal. 5:2). A true relationship with God is a matter of the heart. It is a spiritual thing and not a mark on the body. As the importance of physical circumcision began to diminish, the Bible writers began to speak of "circumcision of the heart." Paul went further to define this spiritual circumcision as "putting off of the sinful nature" (Col. 2:11). As previously a piece of skin was cut loose and taken away, in a like manner the sinful nature was dealt with in the circumcision of the heart.

This new concept brought an end to the idea that salvation was only for the Jews and that essentially all that was required was to conform to a Jewish tradition. What really counts is the destruction of the sinful nature, which is evidenced by a transformed life and the fruit of the Spirit.

God is not interested in ceremony, liturgy, and dead traditions. He looks at the heart instead.

Question for Reflection: Are you merely "going through the motions" in your relationship with God?

52

Freedom from Sin

You have been set free from sin and have become
slaves to righteousness.   —Rom. 6:18

Isn't it interesting that the things you choose to own usually wind up owning you? We buy new cars and then must
work harder than ever to make the payments. We buy new
homes and then must spend our weekends maintaining them.
Even worse is the way our sinful behaviors come to dominate
our lives. One of the cruelest consequences of sin is that it will
make a slave out of you. One of the greatest benefits of
redemption is that it will set you free from sin.

Christ declared that one of the objectives of His coming was
to "set the captives free." Only holiness theology fulfills this promise in the truest sense. A doctrine that allows a person to keep on
sinning leaves him or her in slavery! The Scripture is very clear on
this point: "Don't you know that when you offer yourselves to
someone to obey him as slaves, you are slaves to the one whom
you obey—whether you are slaves to sin, which leads to death, or
to obedience, which leads to righteousness?" (v. 16).

Slavery is a terrible thing, and slavery to sin is the worst
kind. It is hard to believe that our God, who does everything
with such excellence, would offer a salvation that doesn't
solve the problem! To be set free from sin is God's ultimate
goal in His plan for us. He begins by dealing with the problem
of guilt through forgiveness. But the process is not complete
until the Holy Spirit deals with the principle of sin that dwells
in us. Only when that is cleansed by a baptism of fire can we
be said to be fully freed from sin.

John declared the objective of Christ's coming: "The reason the Son of God appeared was to destroy the devil's work"
(1 John 3:8). That is precisely what He did: "For he has rescued
us from the dominion of darkness and brought us into the
kingdom of the Son he loves" (Col. 1:13).

The hymn writer put it well in the hymn "Glorious Freedom":

> *Once I was bound by sin's galling fetters,*
> *Chained like a slave I struggled in vain.*
> *But I received a glorious freedom,*
> *When Jesus broke my fetters in twain.**

Question for Reflection: Have you been set free from sin?

53

A Glorious Slavery

What then? Shall we sin because we are not under law but under grace? By no means! Don't you know that when you offer yourselves to someone to obey him as slaves, you are slaves to the one whom you obey—whether you are slaves to sin, which leads to death, or to obedience, which leads to righteousness? But thanks be to God that, though you used to be slaves to sin, you wholeheartedly obeyed the form of teaching to which you were entrusted. You have been set free from sin and have become slaves to righteousness. —Rom. 6:15–18

Maybe you've heard the commonly used slur against marriage in which one partner refers to the other as "the old ball-and-chain." Happily married folk don't use that epithet, however. They realize that while taking on marriage vows does imply a certain loss of freedom, there is far more to be gained by binding oneself in a loving relationship with a mate. Our relationship with God is much the same. In one sense, it is "slavery" as we are bound to God. Yet it is a slavery that brings glorious freedom from sin.

---

*Haldor Lillenas, Nazarene Publishing House.

There are several biblical texts that refer to the fact that once we have been liberated from the slavery of sin, it is replaced by another kind of slavery—we become slaves to God and righteousness. What does this mean? Has the deliverance we have found from sin only been exchanged for slavery to another master? Not exactly! It is true that when we become committed to obey God, we have surrendered our sovereignty to Him, but this is vastly different.

To begin with, it is a voluntary slavery. Does that sound like a contradiction? Well, it isn't. The slavery of sin is imposed upon us. Our slavery to God results from a free choice motivated by love for Him. The highest use we can make of our power of choice is to relinquish it to God. We commit to it joyfully and gladly because we want to. We receive many benefits from our service to God. One of the great benefits of this glorious slavery is that it "leads to holiness, and the result is eternal life" (v. 22).

Slavery to God is not harsh or degrading. It is a service of love. Our service and obedience is motivated by love. Even on the human level, when we do things for those we love, we do not count it as sacrifice but privilege. There are many wonderful benefits to this relationship, but perhaps the greatest is that it "leads to holiness, and the result is eternal life."

Question for Reflection: Are you a "slave" to Christ?

54

Two Ways of Thinking

Those who live according to the sinful nature have their minds set on what that nature desires; but those who live in accordance with the Spirit have their minds set on what the Spirit desires. The mind of sinful man is death, but the mind controlled by the Spirit is life and peace; the sinful mind is hostile to God. It does not submit to God's law, nor can it do so. Those controlled by the sinful nature cannot please God.

—Rom. 8:5–8

In spiritual terms, the world is divided into two radically opposed camps. There are those who are controlled by the sinful nature and those who are controlled by the Holy Spirit. These two groups are identified by two very different ways of thinking.

The sinful mind is marked by a focus on the desires of the sinful nature. These desires are dominated by appetites of the flesh, things that are temporal, selfishness, and greed.

Those who are controlled by the Spirit are focused on spiritual values, serving others, doing good, and pleasing God.

We are all born with a sinful nature. It may be described as a tendency or inclination toward sin, or a "bent" toward sinning. It is a sad state of corruption in our innermost being. It results in an internal conflict when we try to do what is good or right. It will continue to cause trouble until it is miraculously cleansed by the Holy Spirit.

These two radically different ways of thinking lead to different ends. The sinful mind will inevitably lead to spiritual death (separation from God). The Spirit-controlled mind will lead to life, peace, and eventually to heaven.

One of the sad things about the dominance of the sinful mind is its deceptiveness. It deludes a person into thinking that the temporary satisfaction of the desires of the flesh is better than the way of the Spirit. The truth is that it is the control of the Spirit that leads to real joy and lasting satisfaction.

Question for Reflection: Is your life controlled by the Holy Spirit?

55

Hostility to God

The sinful mind is hostile to God. It does not submit to God's law, nor can it do so. Those controlled by the sinful nature cannot please God.   —Rom. 8:7–8

During an election year, many people try to remain neutral for as long as possible. They want to survey the entire field, listen to all the candidates, and take their time to choose the one they will support. But election day will come sooner or later, forcing a choice. You cannot remain impartial forever.

Likewise there is no possible neutrality in our relationship to God. Ultimately, we are either on His side or against Him. There is no middle ground. The text clearly states that the sinful mind is hostile to God. To put it even more bluntly, the person controlled by the sinful mind has declared himself to be an enemy of God. Can you imagine what that means? It is saying to God, "OK, God, let's go to war against each other." That is ridiculous! In a conflict with God, guess who is going to win! You may be able to have your way for a while, and even shake your clinched fist in the face of God, but eventually God always has the last word.

How can a person be so audacious as to say to God, "You may be God, but I am smarter than You. My way is better than Your way. There are some things You have not learned yet." It is unthinkable to treat God that way. However, in essence that is what a person does when he or she chooses the way of hostility to God. It must be amusing to Almighty God for a tiny little speck of dust in the vast universe to choose to go to war against the Creator of it all. It is the height of all self-deception to think that anybody could win against God.

There is absolutely no way that a sinful mind can submit to the law of God. They are opposites. Incompatible. Contradictory.

Paul's final conclusion on the subject is that because of the hostile nature of the sinful mind, there is no possible way that a person under its control can please God. It is simple logic:

hostility and harmony cannot coexist; pleasing God and pleasing yourself cannot happen simultaneously. Control by the Spirit and control by your evil nature are contradictory. It is your choice, but it must be one way or the other.

Question for Reflection: Have you chosen to follow God?

56

Consecration

> Therefore, I urge you, brothers, in view of God's mercy, to offer your bodies as living sacrifices, holy and pleasing to God—this is your spiritual act of worship. Do not conform any longer to the pattern of this world, but be transformed by the renewing of your mind. Then you will be able to test and approve what God's will is—his good, pleasing and perfect will.   —Rom. 12:1–2

In this digital age, we have become accustomed to the idea of multitasking. We talk on the phone while scanning e-mail. We cook dinner while helping our kids with their homework. We believe that we can direct our attention in two or three directions simultaneously. That may work in managing a workday, but it spells disaster in the quest for holiness. In order to be sanctified by God, we must first be consecrated—that is, totally devoted to Him.

The term "consecration," when applied to personal religious experience, simply means to give something to God. It can apply to many things and to different degrees. Complete consecration means that everything has been given to God without reserve. At this point, a person is eligible for entire sanctification. It is in this condition that the Holy Spirit has permission to move in and take control. The first thing He does is to cleanse the heart from the sinful nature. Then the

Spirit's indwelling presence provides a new source of enabling power to serve God, to live a victorious life, and to act from unselfish and pure motives.

The text is presented against the background of the Old Testament custom of offering burned sacrifices upon an altar in the Temple. In the New Testament, God prefers that we offer ourselves in such a way that we become "living sacrifices." This is an act of worship that pleases God, allows Him to transform our lives by renewal of our way of thinking, and to lead us to His perfect will for our lives. The will of God is always good for us. Consecration is the human part. Entire sanctification is the divine response to our consecration.

One of the reasons why God's sanctifying work takes place in two steps is because it is impossible to consecrate a sinful life. We can only consecrate to God what is fit for His service. You cannot consecrate sin.

Consecration involves renouncing our (imagined) personal sovereignty and letting the Spirit take control. From then on our objective is not to live for our own benefit but for the glory of God.

Question for Reflection: Have you consecrated yourself fully to God?

57

Holiness: The Norm for God's People

I have written you quite boldly on some points, as if to remind you of them again, because of the grace God gave me to be a minister of Christ Jesus to the Gentiles with the priestly duty of proclaiming the gospel of God, so that the Gentiles might become an offering acceptable to God, sanctified by the Holy Spirit.   —Rom. 15:15-16

What was the acceptable standard of achievement when

you went to school? Was everyone expected to be an A student? Was a B considered a "good grade"? Was it your goal to be a C student? In most academic settings, D is considered at least a passing grade and will earn a diploma. The standard for God's people, however, is a bit higher—not in academic terms but spiritually. We are all expected to be holy as He is holy.

We have already seen how heart purity was the essence of what the Holy Spirit did for the Jews at Pentecost. We have also seen how the same thing was repeated for the Gentiles. On the Day of Pentecost, Peter proclaimed the Spirit's cleansing work to be a blessing for the peoples of all nations. This fact was backed up by the miracle of communicating it in the native languages of those who witnessed it.

Once again Paul makes it clear that God's plan is the same for both Jews and Gentiles (those of all other nations). Paul wants the Gentile converts to be "an offering acceptable to God." Then he adds, "sanctified by the Holy Spirit." In the final analysis, that is the only way anyone can be acceptable to God. The word "sanctify" basically means to make holy. Holiness is the norm God wants for all His people.

In his second letter to the Thessalonians, Paul speaks of how "God chose you to be saved through the sanctifying work of the Spirit" (2:13). Entire sanctification is the goal from the very beginning of the work of the Spirit in the human heart. It includes everything that contributes to the goal of making us holy, including conviction, justification, and regeneration (the new birth). We are saved so we can be sanctified! The whole thing is being carried out by "the sanctifying work of the Spirit." There is no other agency that can accomplish this.

Make no mistake about it; God wants us to be holy! No other standard is acceptable. It is the same for all people and for all time. It is the culminating point of God's great plan for our personal salvation. We must not stop until we reach this goal.

Question for Reflection: Is it your goal to be holy?

58

The Guarantee

Now it is God who makes both us and you stand firm in Christ. He anointed us, set his seal of ownership on us, and put his Spirit in our hearts as a deposit, guaranteeing what is to come.   —2 Cor. 1:21–22

We like to get credit for the things we do, but in the case of sanctification we cannot take any credit. Sanctification is the work of God in our lives; it's nothing we can do for ourselves. This text mentions five essential elements of God's action when He brings us into the fullness of His blessing.

1. Establishment: Entire sanctification has been called "the establishing grace." It marks the point at which a previously up-and-down experience with God becomes firm and stable. Falling from grace can often be accounted for by the fact that believers have not pressed on into the deeper experience in which we stand firm in Christ.

2. Anointing: The symbol of anointing is used in different ways in Scripture, but in general it refers to a special enabling. We speak of a preacher delivering a message "under the anointing of the Spirit." It represents the help of the Spirit in carrying out the task assigned to us in God's service.

3. The Sealing: This is the seal by which God identifies us as belonging to Him—the seal of ownership. This ownership is based on the fact that He created us; He redeemed us, and that we have voluntarily given (consecrated) ourselves to Him. Paul focused on this concept when he spoke of "the God whose I am" (Acts 27:23).

4. The gift of the Spirit: The essence of intimacy with God is His Spirit He has put in our hearts. There are many "gifts of the Spirit" (gifts the Spirit gives), but the greatest gift is the Spirit himself.

5. The guarantee: The inheritance of the children of God is only partially realized in this life. It will be fulfilled complete-

ly when we get to heaven. In the meantime He has given us the Spirit as a guarantee of what is yet to come. With the fullness of the Spirit we can enjoy a bit of heaven right here on earth.

Question for Reflection: Have you experienced this work of God in your heart?

59

Separation from the World (Sin)

Therefore come out from them and be separate, says the Lord. Touch no unclean thing, and I will receive you. I will be a Father to you, and you will be my sons and daughters, says the Lord Almighty.
—2 Cor. 6:17–18; see also John 17:6, 11, 14

Most of us don't like to be different. We generally work hard at blending in with those around us. We like to wear clothes that are in style; we like to drive the latest automobiles, and we ruthlessly eliminate the dandelions from our lawn. We want to blend in. But a key concept in both the Old and New Testaments is that God's people should be different. The Jews were constantly urged to separate themselves from the pagan nations around them and to reject their sinful practices and false gods. God's people should be distinctively identifiable by the way they live.

The word "separate" has two dimensions: What a person is separated from and what he or she is separated to. The "separated from" dimension refers to everything sinful. The "separated to" dimension refers to being set apart for God. To be separated from everything sinful is what prepares us to be set apart for God's use. To be separated from impurity means to be pure. To be separated from uncleanness is to be clean. To be separated from sin in act and nature is to be holy.

There are other distinctives about Christians that set them

apart when it comes to behavior. People who have "the mind of Christ" think differently from the world. They see things and people as Jesus sees them.

They talk differently as well. The language they use, as well as the subjects they focus on, separates them from the general public.

The fruit of the Spirit should be in evidence in the lives of Christians.

Christians trust God to see them through the difficult times of life, while unbelievers have no such resource of encouragement.

When facing death those who have hope in Christ for eternal life are in a different category.

Question for Reflection: Are you blending in with the world around you, or are you different?

60

Purify Yourselves

Since we have these promises, dear friends, let us purify ourselves from everything that contaminates body and spirit, perfecting holiness out of reverence for God.   —2 Cor. 7:1

Cleanliness is a critical component of good health. In a hospital the staff is nearly fanatical about keeping things clean and, in the operating suite, sterile. In that setting, contamination kills. Spiritually, we, too, are to purify ourselves. Purification is a critical component of sanctification.

The command to purify ourselves, however, should not be understood to mean this is something that a person can do for himself or herself alone. God alone has the power to purify a sinful heart. But we must cooperate with God in order for Him to do it. The requirements must be met, including renouncing sin, and an in-depth consecration that allows God to work out His will in us. God always acts when we have done our part.

Since we have all these wonderful promises, it would be a shame not to realize their potential. What God has promised, we should all actively seek. His promises are all good and should not be rejected.

Some sins are limited to the realm of the spirit. Others may involve the body. Both are mentioned here to emphasize that we should avoid anything that has a contaminating effect on any part of us. Purity is not real purity until it is complete. There is no such thing as contaminated purity.

The cleansing of the heart is the first step toward "perfecting" holiness in us. There may still be some things the Spirit needs to teach us. There will always be room for spiritual growth toward higher levels of maturity. But after our hearts have been purified, we will act from motives that are good and right. Such acts may not have perfect results, but our intentions will always be good.

Everything that contaminates body or spirit must be avoided. This includes recreation, habits, substances, entertainment, and so forth. You must use discretion, but you must also be honest with yourself.

Question for Reflection: Have you purified yourself for God?

61

Crucified with Christ

I have been crucified with Christ and I no longer live, but Christ lives in me. The life I live in the body, I live by faith in the Son of God, who loved me and gave himself for me.   —Gal. 2:20

The subject of capital punishment is hotly debated in our

society, so it might seem odd that an analogy drawn from execution would be used to describe our new life in Christ. Yet Jesus was put to death by crucifixion, the preferred method of execution in the ancient world, and the apostle Paul borrows that image in describing how we now relate to Christ. We must die spiritually in order to live again.

The idea is that when we enter into union with Christ, it identifies us with His death. That is to say, we die with Christ. This is more than a figure of speech. By faith we make Christ's death our own and visualize ourselves dying with Christ.

That is why Paul can say, "I no longer live, but Christ lives in me." He is testifying to the fact that he has voluntarily surrendered his will or his right to personal sovereignty. He is saying that since he died with Christ, he is no longer alive. His life has been taken over by Christ and is being lived under Christ's guidance and governance. Christ has taken over his life in such a way that it is no longer Paul's life but Christ's life being lived out through him.

If you follow through on the same rationale of his identification with Christ's death, it also applies to His resurrection. His death with Christ is what opens the door to new-resurrection life.

Now, this crucifixion with Christ is not to be confused with the self-crucifixion of the sinful nature. That is completely different. It is the old sinful depraved nature that dies (5:24).

There are many benefits to this new life, but the source of it all is found in the love of Christ, "who loved me and gave himself for me."

Can you say that you are so committed to Christ that you are no longer living your life, but it is Christ that is living in you? It is one way of saying that your decisions are being made by Christ. You are allowing Him to live His life through you. This is possible because you have surrendered your will to His.

Question for Reflection: Have you died with Christ?

62

The Crucifixion of the Sinful Nature

> Those who belong to Christ Jesus have crucified the sinful nature with its passions and desires. Since we live by the Spirit, let us keep in step with the Spirit. Let us not become conceited, provoking and envying each other. —Gal. 5:24–26

What solutions have you tried for dealing with the problem of sin in your life? Willpower? Counseling? Accountability partners? Each of these measures may be helpful in living out our resolve to follow Christ, but for dealing with sin there is only one real solution—execution. The Bible uses very strong language when it comes to telling how to deal with the sinful nature. It cannot be tolerated, pampered, or excused. The only way it can be effectively dealt with is to be put to death by crucifixion.

Physical death by crucifixion is very painful, and nobody in his or her right mind would ever willingly submit to it. When the sinful nature is confronted with the possibility of being crucified, it goes to extremes to avoid it! It will even promise to be good and behave more acceptably. The sinful mind may even promise to submit to God's law, but it cannot keep the promise, because by nature it is hostile to God. The only way to be freed from it is to put it to death!

There is an interesting symbolism here. When a person dies he or she ceases to respond to the environment around him or her. In other words, a dead person cannot be tempted. You may bring in delicious food, melodious music, masterful art, or anything else desirable, but it brings no response from a dead person. A cadaver just lies there without even a smile or a twitch. When the sinful nature has been crucified, it no longer responds to sinful attractions, because it has become a spiritual mind. The cleansing of the Holy Spirit has broken the power of sin. Paul stated it this way: "For we know that our old self was crucified with him so that the body of sin might be done away with ["rendered powerless" (margin)]" (Rom. 6:6).

There is another interesting concept in this text: Paul advises, "Let us keep in step with the Spirit." In submission to the guidance of the Spirit, we should neither run ahead nor lag behind His directions. It is a picture of a daily walk with Him in close harmony and fellowship. This is the exact opposite of trying to walk with God while the sinful mind is still active.

Question for Reflection: Has the sinful nature been put to death in you?

63

God's Original Choice for Us

For he chose us in him before the creation of the world to be holy and blameless in his sight.

—Eph. 1:4

What is the longest-range plan you've ever made? Perhaps you determined to graduate from high school or college, and it took four full years to do it, perhaps longer. It could be that you decided to save up money for a grand celebration of your 10- or 20-year anniversary. Maybe you took on a 30-year mortgage and finally paid it off. That's a long time. Yet God's plan for your sanctification has taken even longer—it all started before the world began.

Somewhere in the immeasurable "eternal present" of God He made a choice. He decided to create a new creature like nothing that had ever existed before. He wanted to enjoy love and fellowship with this creature, but for that to happen He would have to endow this new being with the power to make free choices. It would be a great adventure, but it also involved some risks. (What good would fellowship be if it was forced?)

Now, God had a detailed plan in mind. He wanted human beings to have certain characteristics in common with Him to make real fellowship possible. He also chose that we should be "holy and blameless in his sight." That was God's choice. Please note that since God's purposes are unchangeable, His choice for humankind then will always be true. Adam and Eve, exercising their freedom, made some bad choices and thereby introduced sin to the human race. But then, in His great mercy and love, God came up with another plan; a plan to redeem the human race and to recover that which had been lost in Eden. The goals were exactly the same as in the beginning: a race of people who were holy and blameless, a people who would be re-created in the likeness of God. This would make possible once again a condition of peace and harmony with the Creator and restore the fellowship that had been broken by the intrusion of sin.

The word "holy" refers to the inner quality of human nature or character. "Blameless" on the other hand relates to our obedience and outward behavior. Both are important to God. Both are included in the provision Christ made on the Cross. Both are an attainable reality for all believers.

Nothing less will ever satisfy God. He will never be able to enjoy fellowship with a sinful heart or a disobedient rebel. His first choice will forever remain as the standard for His people.

Question for Reflection: Are you focused on the long-range goal of living a holy life?

64

All the Fullness of God

I pray that out of his glorious riches he may strengthen you with power through his Spirit in your inner being, so that Christ may dwell in your hearts through faith. And I pray that you, being rooted and established in love, may have power, together with all the saints, to grasp how wide and long and high and deep is the love of Christ, and to know this love that surpasses knowledge—that you may be filled to the measure of all the fullness of God.   —Eph. 3:16–19

What is your highest goal for yourself? Do you hope someday to master a musical instrument? Learn a new language? Own your own company? Whatever your highest aim, no doubt it falls far short of God's highest aim for you—that you become like Him.

The scripture above is part of a prayer that Paul prayed for the Ephesians. All of his petitions for them are interesting, but the last one is one of those scriptures that just "blows your mind." Let's look at what he asks for them:

- That they be strengthened in their "inner being"
- That Christ may dwell in their hearts
- That they be rooted and established in love
- That they grasp the dimensions of Christ's love
- That they be filled with all the fullness of God

They all have important implications, but for lack of space we will deal only with the last one.

It seems almost incredible that a weak, mortal, human being could contain "all the fullness of God." This just has to be the maximum experience attainable by a human. God has gone beyond everything that is reasonable and has given all of himself to us without limitation. It would take more than a lifetime to plumb the depths of what that means. What a deal that is! Yes, God wants all of us, but in exchange He gives all of himself to us. It is beyond our imagination.

What is included in "all the fullness of God"? It must include all His goodness, all His power, all His wisdom, all His holiness, all His blessings, all His will, and all His love. You name it—it's all there. It is a fantastic potential. The question is to what degree do these words describe your experience of God?

Question for Reflection: Are you being filled with "all the fullness of God"?

65

Created to Be like God

You were taught, with regard to your former way of life, to put off your old self, which is being corrupted by its deceitful desires; to be made new in the attitude of your minds; and to put on the new self, created to be like God in true righteousness and holiness.
—Eph. 4:22–24

Transformation is a wonderful thing. You have perhaps witnessed this phenomenon in nature, as a lowly caterpillar is transformed into a beautiful butterfly. We sometimes say that neighborhoods or cities that are dramatically revitalized are "transformed." Transformation is nothing less than complete change—from one thing into another. And transformation is God's goal for you.

This text speaks to us about radical transformation. The "old self" is characterized by "corruption and deceitful desires." But when God re-creates a new self to replace the old one, it is described as "created to be like God." The contrast could not be greater: from corruption and deceit to godliness.

This in-depth change involves a renewal of the mind. The new self thinks very differently than it did under the old regime. There is a change of focus as Paul describes it: "Finally, brothers, whatever is true, whatever is noble, whatever is right, whatever is pure, whatever is lovely, whatever is admirable—if anything is excellent or praiseworthy—think about such things" (Phil. 4:8). The new way of thinking is in stark contrast to the old under the influences of "deceitful desires."

Two characteristics of godliness are mentioned: Righteousness, which is understood to be right living, the ethical aspect of the Christian life—obedience to God's laws, and holiness, which is the internal change of nature, the miracle of how God imparts His nature to a human heart. The real change takes place on the inside, but it manifests itself externally in our daily lives.

This transformation completes the cycle. We were originally made "in the image of God." Unfortunately, we lost that image. But under God's redemptive plan, we are re-created once more "to be like God."

In this sense the mission of Christ "to seek and to save what was lost" (Luke 19:10) was fulfilled when the new plan restored the potential to recover what was lost.

Question for Reflection: Have you been transformed?

66

Filled with the Holy Spirit

Do not get drunk on wine, which leads to debauchery. Instead, be filled with the Spirit.   —Eph. 5:18

It was an incredible day! The Day of Pentecost, when the Holy Spirit was poured out upon believers, was one of the most powerful, incredible, and exciting moments in the history of the Church. Exactly what happened on that day? Numerous words are used to describe what happened to the disciples: "purified," "cleansed," "sanctified," and "baptized with the Holy Spirit." One of the most descriptive is the phrase "filled with the Holy Spirit." Let us look at some of the implications of this figure of speech.

Before a vessel can be filled with anything, it must first be emptied of any other substance. Likewise, there is both a negative and a positive aspect to the fullness of the Spirit. Before He can fill a heart and make it holy, all that is unholy must be removed. All sinful pride and selfishness must go, along with habits and attitudes that do not glorify God. The Holy Spirit will not dwell in a heart that is contaminated by anything sinful. Once the heart is free from contaminating influences, the Holy Spirit may enter in His fullness and take up His abode.

When the Holy Spirit fills a heart, it means there is no longer a conflict over who is in control.

"Filled" suggests completeness. If a jar has been filled with something, there is no more room for anything else to be poured into it. When the Holy Spirit fills, it means we have all of Him, but we do not get all of Him until He has all of us.

It is interesting that there is a negative comparison between being filled with the Spirit and being drunk. You may remember that at Pentecost some of the observers accused the disciples of being drunk. Of course, that was not true, but the filling with the Holy Spirit did affect their behavior in ways the world could not understand or explain. The enthusiasm and joy of Spirit-filled Christians is still a mystery to the world.

Finally, note that this is a command, not a suggestion. It is a part of God's plan we should all seek to experience.

Question for Reflection: Have you been filled with the Spirit?

67

Cleansed, Without Stain or Blemish

Husbands, love your wives, just as Christ loved the church and gave himself up for her to make her holy, cleansing her by the washing with water through the word, and to present her to himself as a radiant church, without stain or wrinkle or any other blemish, but holy and blameless. —Eph. 5:25–27

The marriage relationship makes a wonderful analogy for our relationship with God. The metaphor is so apt that the apostle Paul made use of it in Scripture! In Ephesians Paul began by giving advice to husbands about how they should love their wives. He compared it to Christ's love for the Church. What a message to husbands! But before finishing the sentence, Paul changed his focus to the nature of the Church. The characteristics of the Church that Paul mentions also apply to those who compose the Church. The characteristics of the Church cannot be different from the characteristics of those who make it up. Look at the characteristics he mentions: holy, cleansed, radiant, without stain, without wrinkles, without blemish, blameless. What a challenge to be a part of a Church like that! The standards for the Church are without compromise.

The wonderful Church described by Paul is also known as the Bride of Christ. It is inconceivable that Christ would be united to a "bride" that would have the slightest hint of contamination or sin of any kind. She must be clean, pure, and radiant in every way. The slightest stain or blemish would disqualify her from the high position of being the Bride of Christ. All of those who aspire to be a part of the true and glorious Church must have the same ideals. No exceptions!

That sets the standard very high, but make no mistake about it, it is attainable. Every requirement of God is accompanied by the necessary grace to achieve it.

We have no way of knowing for sure who belongs to the real (invisible) Church. But God keeps good records, and the day will come when the wrinkles, stains, and blemishes will be removed.

Question for Reflection: Are you part of Christ's holy bride, the Church?

68

Mature Christians

All of us who are mature should take such a view of things. And if on some point you think differently, that too God will make clear to you. Only let us live up to what we have already attained.   —Phil. 3:15–16

Think of the ways you have changed over the course of your life. As a child, you were no doubt smaller and weaker than you are now. As a teenager, you may have been a bit carefree, even reckless at times. As you grew up, you matured. You changed into a wiser, stronger, more productive person. That same phenomenon—growing to maturity—should characterize you spiritually as well.

We must distinguish between purity and maturity. Here are some of the ways they are different:
- Cleansing takes place in a moment. Maturity develops over many years.
- Purity is a condition of the heart. Maturity is related to wisdom and knowledge.
- A Christian may have a pure heart and still be immature. A person may grow in degrees of maturity, but not in purity (the heart is either pure or not pure).
- A person may have a pure heart and at the same time be unwise in some of the things he or she does.

The ideal is to start with a pure heart and then to be constantly growing toward maturity. Progress in maturity never stops.

There are some ministries in the Church that, in most cases, are best assigned to mature Christians. Some positions of leadership, counseling, and teaching require higher levels of maturity. In most cases, mature Christians will have learned some life lessons that make them wiser and more stable. The important thing is to keep moving ahead and to constantly build on what we have already attained.

It is not shameful to be a newborn baby, but it does indicate that something is wrong when after years of experience normal people are still carrying around the baby bottles and pacifiers. It is a good idea to measure our maturity level occasionally.

Question for Reflection: Are you maturing in Christ?

69

The Purpose of Christ's Death

Once you were alienated from God and were enemies in your minds because of your evil behavior. But now he has reconciled you by Christ's physical body through death to present you holy in his sight, without blemish and free from accusation.   —Col. 1:21–22

Have you ever been under suspicion for something? It's a terrible feeling to be thought guilty for wrongdoing. And in the case of sin, we are not only under suspicion but also guilty. For all have sinned! That makes our new position in Christ even more incredible, for we are now reconciled to God and free from suspicion.

What a contrast there is in this verse! It starts with being alienated from God, moves on to becoming an enemy of God, then proceeds to reconciliation with God, culminates in being made holy, and ends up in freedom from accusation. It goes from a very sad beginning and moves through all of the steps to the final goal for us to be made holy with no grounds for an accusation against us.

We are reminded here once again that all of the wonderful blessings contained in this verse have been purchased for us through the death of Christ. That is the source of all blessings and benefits.

This is an interesting insight: when God prepares to present us holy, we are free from accusation. Who might want to make an accusation against us? Satan? Another human being who is our enemy? The point is that when we have been judged and approved by God, all other opinions are irrelevant. If God does not condemn us, it makes no difference what others might say. The right to judge belongs exclusively to God who sees our hearts and knows our motives and intentions. We do not have to worry about accusations from any other source. Being right in the sight of God is all that counts. Only God has the final word regarding our righteousness.

The freedom from accusation is liberating. It brings to mind the conversation Jesus had with the adulteress woman being accused in John 8:4–11. Jesus had written something on the ground that sent her accusers slinking away. When there was no one left to accuse her, Jesus said, "Neither do I condemn you. . . . Go now and leave your life of sin" (v. 11). She was free from accusation.

Question for Reflection: How does your newfound freedom in Christ affect your behavior?

70

Readiness for Christ's Return

May he strengthen your hearts so that you will be blameless and holy in the presence of our God and Father when our Lord Jesus comes with all his holy ones.   —1 Thess. 3:13

The return of Christ has been the subject of speculation for thousands of years. Many Christians are preoccupied with the questions of where, when, and how Christ will appear again on the earth. The subject is treated by a seemingly endless number of sermons, books, and movies. However, the most important question concerning the Second Coming is discussed very little; namely, how shall we be prepared for Christ's return?

It really doesn't make a lot of difference when it will happen or the circumstances that will accompany it, but it will make a tremendous difference whether or not we are ready. It is very important that we understand the only condition that will be acceptable on that day. This text answers that question clearly and unmistakably: we must be "blameless and holy."

Blamelessness teaches us that we must have no guilt. Guilt results from willful sinning. It can only be remedied by forgiveness that results in justification. Holiness results from cleansing, which is the work of the Holy Spirit. Both of these steps are important. Blamelessness means we are not liable for punishment for the sins we have committed in the past. Holiness gives us the right to enter heaven where nothing that contaminates will be allowed (Rev. 21:27).

Take note that when Christ returns He will come with all the saints who have gone before. They are described as "all his holy ones." Is this not evidence that all those who made it to heaven were holy people?

This verse is actually in the form of a prayer for those to whom Paul was writing. He asks that God strengthen them so they will be ready. Strength is needed in order to have a firm resolve to be faithful to the end, to not yield when tempted, and to not give up when weary in the battle. The resources are both adequate and available for us to be ready when He calls or comes. The catch is that we have no way of knowing when He will come. However, this is no problem if we live the life of holiness continually.

Question for Reflection: What will you need to do in order to be ready for Christ's return?

71

The Will of God

> It is God's will that you should be sanctified: that you should avoid sexual immorality; that each of you should learn to control his own body in a way that is holy and honorable. —1 Thess. 4:3–4

Are you trying to find and follow God's will for your life? Most Christians would say that they are. What they usually mean is that they are trying to find and enter the life path or vocation that God has in mind for them. Or they may be facing a major life decision and are intent on making the choice that is most pleasing to God. Yet there is another way to think of God's will, one that involves your sanctification.

There is nothing more important in your life than finding and fulfilling God's will. His will may fall into several different categories: (1) His will for you in a specific situation. Example: Your lifework or whom you should marry. (2) His permissive will. Example: What He allows but does not require. (3) His general will. In the first two cases, His will may be different for every individual. In the third case, it is the same for everyone.

In some cases, it may not be easy to determine His will,

but in other cases it takes no effort at all, for He has clearly declared it in His Word. In two fundamental issues there can be no mistake about it. (1) He wants everyone to be saved (Matt. 18:14). (2) He wants everyone to be sanctified (see text above). Since, in these cases, He has made it so clear in His Word what His will is, it should be a matter of serious concern for every Christian.

It would be the height of folly to reject God's will. After all, He is our Creator. He has the right to claim our obedience. We should also consider the purpose of His will, which is to bless us, do what is best for us, and fit us for heaven.

When God says, "I want to sanctify you," what could possibly be a valid reason for either ignoring His desire or rejecting it? To reject His will must be either because we think our knowledge is superior to His or that we are in open rebellion against His will. Both of these excuses are irrational. The only reasonable response to the will of God is: "Lord, I want Your will to be done in me. Do whatever You need to do to make me what You want me to be." To fall short of holiness of heart is a sure way to miss God's will! It would be a tragedy to miss it, for God's will is always the best for us. You can't improve on His will for you.

Question for Reflection: What is God's will for your life?

72

The Call to a Holy Life

For God did not call us to be impure, but to live a holy life. Therefore, he who rejects this instruction does not reject man but God, who gives you his Holy Spirit. —1 Thess. 4:7–8

How did you become a Christian? Did you find God or did God find you? Most of us would admit the truth on this point, which is that we were far from God when He came looking for us. The same is true in sanctification. We are made holy by God's initiative. He does not expect us to search blindly for it. He calls us to it. The call comes in various ways. He calls us through His Word, through the influence of the Holy Spirit, and through His servants He calls to preach it. His call from any of these sources may be rejected. But the call from any of these sources comes from God, and to reject it is a direct rejection of God himself. Any person should think very seriously before rejecting a call that comes from heaven. To reject God's call to holiness is to reject heaven. Who would want to do that?

This call goes deeper than to simply subscribe to a doctrine or a creed. It is a call to radical transformation. It begins as an internal transformation—a cleansing, a change of nature. Then it is worked out on the playing field of everyday life. It is not valid if it does not affect the way we live.

I have frequently asked people to describe in one word the kind of life they are striving to live. The responses have been many and varied: happy, prosperous, pleasurable, and so forth. Seldom have I heard the word "holy" used. However, this is the biblical standard for all Christians. Can you say that living a holy life is your highest aspiration? As far as God is concerned, that is the only adequate response. There is no other way to please Him.

There is an interesting comment in the chapter following the text above. It says, "The one who calls you is faithful and he will do it" (5:24). This assures us that the One who calls us will do His part for the person who responds to His call. If you purpose in your heart to live a holy life, you can count on God's help. He has called you to it and He will help you achieve what He has called you to.

Question for Reflection: Have you responded to God's call to holiness?

73

A Thorough Job

May God himself, the God of peace, sanctify you through and through. May your whole spirit, soul and body be kept blameless at the coming of our Lord Jesus Christ.   —1 Thess. 5:23

The Holy Spirit will not just partially heal the deep spiritual wound of sin. His work in your life will be thorough and complete. The text uses very powerful language to express the in-depth, radical, complete nature of the work of the Holy Spirit in the human heart. It is not a casual, superficial, half-hearted, or partial operation. It is more like major surgery that gets to the bottom of the problem and solves it.

"Through and through" suggests an action that is complete and effective. Holiness and sin are incompatible. They cannot coexist simultaneously in the same heart. Partial remedies are not acceptable. God does not deal in hocus-pocus or fantasy. His solutions are real and deal effectively with the problem.

God deals not only with the "depth" of the problem but also in what we might call the "breadth" of it. He includes "spirit, soul and body." This phrase includes all there is of a person. There is no part of our being that is left out.

Sin has had a broad effect on the human race. It has affected the spirit, soul, and body of humankind. It is reasonable to expect that a solution worthy of God would touch all three of these human dimensions.

Everything God does is done in an excellent and generous way. It is obvious in creation. This characteristic of His nature also carries over into the salvation He planned for humankind. It is totally adequate for every need of every human being. The writer to the Hebrews described it as a "great salvation." It goes beyond treating symptoms and gets to the cause.

His grace is sufficient to completely solve the problem of

sin. "But where sin increased, grace increased all the more" (Rom. 5:20).

Question for Reflection: Has God's work been made complete in you?

74

The Sanctifying Work of the Holy Spirit

But we ought always to thank God for you, brothers loved by the Lord, because from the beginning God chose you to be saved through the sanctifying work of the Spirit and through belief in the truth.

—2 Thess. 2:13

If you have a garage, then you've probably had to tackle the demanding chore of cleaning it out on at least one occasion. That probably took several steps to complete. First, you had to take everything out. Next, you thoroughly cleaned the garage itself. Then you put all the good things back in good order. The entire process may take several Saturdays to complete and is in fact an ongoing task. From that point on, you likely became more vigilant about keeping the garage clean so you wouldn't lose the value of all your labor. In the same way, the work of the Holy Spirit to sanctify us is not a single act performed once for life. Rightly understood the work of sanctifying is both a process and a definite act, or work, of God.

God will work with different people in different ways. His work we know is always the same in act and results. It is an instantaneous act of God (like the new birth or the baptism with the Holy Spirit). We call it "entire sanctification" when the heart is cleansed from the sinful nature in the baptism with the Holy Spirit because at that point the problem of sin is resolved. It always is a process of God working with each of us to bring us to the place where we are willing to see the need to die out to self-centeredness. After we have been cleansed by the Holy Spirit of all sin, there is a continued process of walking in the light as we mature in our relationship with Christ. This is all the work of the Holy Spirit. There is no salvation apart from the Holy Spirit. He is the One who executes the work of God in us from beginning to end.

He is the One who infuses us with new spiritual life in response to our repentance and faith in Christ. But that is just a prerequisite for the next stage of sanctification, which is the cleansing from the sinful nature. Technically, initial sanctification begins in the new birth and later becomes "entire" when the sinful nature is cleansed and the Spirit in His fullness comes to dwell in the heart.

The text also adds another statement to the work of the Spirit: "and through belief in the truth." This does not mean that a seeker for holiness must fully understand all of the theological intricacies of the work of the Spirit to seek it and enjoy it. But it certainly makes it easier to seek for the experience when it makes rational sense. This comes from a sincere search of God's Word, and the godly counsel of those who have experienced it and preach it. It is difficult for a person to seek an experience when there exists doubts about its reality.

Question for Reflection: Where are you in the process of sanctification?

75

Useful for Service

In a large house there are articles not only of gold and silver, but also of wood and clay; some are for noble purposes and some for ignoble. If a man cleanses himself from the latter, he will be an instrument for noble purposes, made holy, useful to the Master and prepared to do any good work.　　—2 Tim. 2:20–21

What is the purpose of my life? Nearly everyone wonders about that question at some point. Big questions like that—questions that get at ultimate meaning—are the stuff of philosophy courses and dramatic novels. Yet in Scripture the answers seem remarkably clear. Life in this world has two major purposes.

The first purpose is to fulfill the requirements for salvation that will qualify a person to enter heaven. Life is a period of probation during which a person must make decisions and take actions, which will determine his or her destiny. That, of course, is of supreme importance. However, there is more to it than that.

A second purpose for life is that God has determined to carry out His plans and purposes in this world through the Church—His holy people. It is interesting that the preparation for both of these purposes is the same: cleansed and "made holy." To become an instrument for noble purposes and useful to the Master and prepared to do any good work requires holiness.

There are several reasons for it. To begin with, God cannot trust a person with a sinful nature to carry out His work. His instruments must be cleansed for the same reason a surgeon cannot operate with contaminated surgical instruments. If he or she tried, it would only spread the disease or increase the infection. You cannot trust the sinful nature.

Besides that, the sinful nature is destructive and unpredictable. You never know what it might do. Chances are, it will rise up at a critical moment and manifest itself in anger, bitterness, jealousy, selfishness, or many other destructive attitudes that would cause havoc in the Church.

We also understand that God's work often requires a power that goes beyond human resources. The needed power comes from the Spirit that dwells in you. It is "'not by might nor power, but by my Spirit,' says the LORD Almighty" (Zech. 4:6). If you want to be an instrument useful to the Master, seek first the fullness of the Holy Spirit.

Question for Reflection: What is the purpose of your life? Is it being achieved?

76

How to Live in This Present Age

For the grace of God that brings salvation has appeared to all men. It teaches us to say "No" to ungodliness and worldly passions, and to live self-controlled, upright and godly lives in this present age, while we wait for the blessed hope—the glorious appearing of our great God and Savior, Jesus Christ, who gave himself for us to redeem us from all wickedness and to purify for himself a people that are his very own, eager to do what is good.

—Titus 2:11–14

We live in a wicked age. Not that it is anything new, for sin has been rampantly beating a destructive path in the world throughout human history. But it certainly seems to be getting worse in our society. As moral restraints are cast aside, wickedness seems to increase like a mighty, destructive, raging river. The question is, How should we live in an age like this?

Titus gives us a few clues. To begin with, we need to learn to say "NO!" to ungodliness and worldly passions. It is really quite simple; just say "NO!" We must take a stand against the current of the spirit of the age. We do not need to get sucked into it! The grace of God is sufficient to keep us unstained by the filthiness and corruption that surrounds us. As Jesus reminded us, we are in the world, but we must not let the world get into us.

He does mention that the times will require us to exercise some discipline and self-control to maintain godly and upright lives. But with the help God offers us, we can do it.

We need to keep in mind that this present wicked age is only temporary. We are only waiting for the blessed hope that our glorious Lord will appear and change everything. That ought to encourage us to "hang in there." Better things are coming! We are on the winning side! Our victory is assured!

Question for Reflection: How good are you at saying "NO" to ungodliness?

77

Two Steps to Holiness

But when the kindness and love of God our Savior appeared, he saved us, not because of righteous things we had done, but because of his mercy. He saved us through the washing of rebirth and renewal by the Holy Spirit, whom he poured out on us generously through Jesus Christ our Savior.   —Titus 3:4–6

Most of us like instant results for just about everything, and we're impatient with things that seem to take more time than is needed. "Can I send you this document electronically? That'll save me a trip." "Can you change the oil on my car at the same time you rotate the tires? That'll be faster." "Why do I have to brush and floss my teeth?" It seems we're always in a hurry.

So the question is sometimes asked as to why God doesn't complete the work of cleansing the sinful nature when He saves us. Well, the limitation is not on God's part, but on ours. These two works of God are so different in nature, and in the conditions required, that it would be psychologically impossible for a person to handle both of these steps simultaneously. Let's compare the two experiences.

The Problem
The New Birth: Guilt has been acquired as a result of willfully committed sins.
Entire Sanctification: Depravity has resulted from the fall of the human race.
Comparison: Two totally different problems

The Solution

The New Birth: Guilt can be resolved only by forgiveness.
Entire Sanctification: Depravity must be dealt with by a cleansing of the sinful nature.
Comparison: Two totally different solutions

The Requirement

The New Birth: Repentance of sins and faith in Christ
Entire Sanctification: A complete consecration that allows the Holy Spirit to fill and take control
Comparison: Two totally different requirements

The Result

The New Birth: Justification (forgiveness)
Entire Sanctification: A pure heart (cleansing)
Comparison: Two totally different results

The twofold nature of sin requires two different solutions. Guilt is resolved only by forgiveness. The sinful nature can be resolved only by cleansing. It is important that they occur in the proper sequence. Since total consecration is the condition for cleansing, it cannot happen while we are still under condemnation for the sins we have committed. Otherwise, we would have to consecrate a life of sin. Unthinkable!

When the Holy Spirit does His work of convicting of sin (making us conscious of our guilt for committed sins and our lost condition), it becomes an overwhelming burden. Our focus at that point is totally on how to get rid of the burden of guilt. It is only later that we discover that even after this guilt is gone, there is still a conflict on the inside. It can be described as a "civil war." It is an inclination toward evil that goes against our good intentions. At this point we refocus our attention on the need to be delivered from the tendency toward sin.

We can compare the situation to an automobile with a steering mechanism that is out of alignment. It is a struggle to keep it on the road because it is constantly pulling toward the ditch at the edge of the road. It requires an adjustment to make it run smoothly in parallel to the white line (holiness).

Question for Reflection: Have you received the second work of grace?

78

A Rest for the People of God

There remains, then, a Sabbath-rest for the people of God; for anyone who enters God's rest also rests from his own work, just as God did from his. Let us, therefore, make every effort to enter that rest, so that no one will fall by following their example of disobedience. —Heb. 4:9–11; see also Ps. 95:7–8

Ah, weekends! It seems that every working person feels the draw of Friday, the end of the workweek and the official start of the weekend, a time for relaxation and recreation. Wouldn't it be odd if one developed the habit of working hard all week but never taking a day off to rest? Life would become drudgery, and we would miss out on a wonderful experience—the Sabbath rest.

That Sabbath rest is a spiritual as well as a physical experience, one created by God for His people. Theologians believe that this rest is what happens when a person gives up the struggle to attain holiness by his or her own efforts and surrenders to let God do it His way. Previous to this surrender there has been a constant conflict and frustrating struggle as the two natures oppose each other. Paul describes it in Rom. 7.

There are two opposing forces within the heart. There is the side that wants to obey and please God, but there is also present the sinful nature that opposes it. It is warfare! The two forces are incompatible. They cannot peaceably coexist. Only one can triumph over the other. It is a struggle to death.

But when victory finally comes, it results in a peace that passes understanding. The war is over, and it is time to rest—

rest from your own works and from the continual internal conflict.

This state of spiritual rest is so desirable that we are urged to "make every effort" to enter it. It is worth whatever it may cost. It is actually anticipatory of the rest we will get in heaven where the forces of evil and conflict will be forever banished. It is this state of rest that has an establishing effect that will in turn provide a safeguard against falling into disobedience.

It is called a Sabbath rest because it is compared to creation. After the creation was completed, the crowning work of God was to provide rest for His people. Sabbath rest is achievable through entire sanctification in this life, but it will be a constant state in heaven.

Question for Reflection: Are you skipping the Sabbath experience that God has created for you?

79

On to Maturity

Therefore let us leave the elementary teachings about Christ and go on to maturity, not laying again the foundation of repentance from acts that lead to death, and of faith in God, instruction about baptisms, the laying on of hands, the resurrection of the dead, and eternal judgment. And God permitting, we will do so.   —Heb. 6:1–3

Everybody likes babies. They bring joy into the world with their arrival. Their presence alone is enough to make children giggle, parents smile, and grandparents burst with joy. The same joy is experienced when new life is formed in Christ. The arrival of a "baby Christian" brings joy on earth and a celebration in heaven. Yet we know that babies won't remain infants for long. It would be odd indeed to see a 10-year-old baby. Likewise, new Christians are intended to "go on" to maturity—and there's something wrong when they don't.

Every healthy church needs to have Christians in all stages of development. If every believer stayed in the stage of spiritual infancy, who would be the teachers? Paul was frustrated by some he said should have been teachers, but they themselves still needed teachers of elementary things (5:12). The church needs strong Christians who have become the pillars of the church.

It is good for all of us occasionally to check up on our spiritual growth. You might ask, where am I on my spiritual journey now in relation to where I was a year ago? Or, how long have I been saved? Isn't it about time for me to be seeking entire sanctification? My observation has been that the gap between initial salvation and entire sanctification is generally much longer than it needs to be.

I urge you in the words of Paul, "Let us . . . go on to maturity."

Question for Reflection: What is the state of your progress in growing toward maturity in Christ?

80

Complete Salvation

Therefore he is able to save completely those who come to God through him, because he always lives to intercede for them.   —Heb. 7:25

Can you imagine a lifeguard who goes after a drowning man and pulls him halfway to shore, then goes about bragging about how he saved him? What about a fireman who bursts into a burning building, picks up a frightened child, then carries that child only halfway out of the house? That would be unthinkable! In order for the rescue to be complete, the person must be brought all the way to safety.

It is the same with your salvation from sin. The words "salvation" or "saved" carry with them the idea of being rescued. In that sense, any salvation that is partial or incomplete is no salvation at all. The writer to the Hebrews is speaking here about how Christ is able to save completely. We often refer to it as the gospel of full salvation. It is a salvation that really does rescue us from evil. Full salvation really does deal with the problem of sin in all of its forms and delivers us from it. A salvation that leaves us in sin is an oxymoron. The two terms contradict each other.

God's kind of salvation is perfect. There is nothing lacking. There is no way to get more saved.

Anything less than complete salvation is not worthy of our God or of Christ's work on the Cross. As you search through the Bible, you will discover that the terminology supports the idea of maximum salvation. We should greatly rejoice in this fact and make sure that when we talk about salvation, we present it in all of its glory.

Full salvation covers all sin for all people. It is a complete solution to our greatest problem. There is no way that we could improve on God's plan to rescue us. No corners have been cut, and no exceptions have been made. The provisions are totally efficacious. There is nothing lacking, nothing that has not been provided for.

Question for Reflection: Are you fully saved from sin?

81

Being Made Holy

Because by one sacrifice he has made perfect forever those who are being made holy.   —Heb. 10:14

"Are we there yet?" Every parent hears those words at

least a few times during a long car trip. Children are impatient for the result and often pay little attention to the landmarks that may be passed along the way. We, too, can be impatient for entire sanctification as if that were the end of a journey. In reality, sanctification itself is a journey that will last for eternity, and there are several important milestones along the way.

Holiness of heart begins at the moment a person turns from sin through repentance and in faith in Christ, which is the first step in the process. Holiness of heart takes another big step forward when the Holy Spirit cleanses the heart from the sinful nature in entire sanctification. At this point the work of the Holy Spirit is perfect and complete as it relates to sin in the heart. However, He is not through yet. He will continue to work with us in the process of becoming more like Christ. That, too, is a part of the process of "being made holy." It goes on throughout life in the broadest sense. It happens in many different ways.

As we go along, we will acquire more knowledge about God and the Bible. As we do, what we learn may reveal that we need to modify our behavior in some way. This doesn't mean we have backslidden and need to get saved again. The Bible refers to this experience as "walking in the light." It means continuous obedience. Even though our cleansing was complete in the baptism with the Holy Spirit, it needs to be kept up to date by continuous obedience. In that sense we continue to "be made holy."

Then there is the matter of tests and trials that come from God. We sometimes find ourselves in a situation where God is proving our loyalty. This happened to Abraham when his faith was severely tested because God asked him to sacrifice his son Isaac. It happened to Job on the bed of affliction when he lost everything he had. A time of testing can turn out in two ways: it can turn out well when we respond to it in the proper way, or we may fail the test. If we are successful in the time of testing, it will make us stronger. Through the experience we may say that we are continuing to "be made holy."

Our final holiness is not guaranteed just because we achieved it at one point. The cleansing is continuous as we walk in the light and through life's experiences we continue to "be made holy."

Question for Reflection: Do you view holiness as a destination or as a journey?

82

The Purpose of God's Discipline

Our fathers disciplined us for a little while as they thought best; but God disciplines us for our good, that we may share in his holiness. No discipline seems pleasant at the time, but painful. Later on, however, it produces a harvest of righteousness and peace for those who have been trained by it.

—Heb. 12:10–11

We could debate whether it is best for parents to correct their children by spanking them or by giving them "time out." But we would probably all agree that parents must discipline their children in some way. Loving parents care about the development of their children, and they exercise discipline in order to correct and properly form their character. Your Heavenly Father does the same.

Earthly fathers, of course, have limited human judgment. Sometimes they are right, on other occasions they may be unjust or abusive. "But God" is different. He never makes a mistake. He always acts in our favor. His objective is always what is good for us.

There is one thing that is for our good above all others: "to share in his holiness." There is only one source of holiness. It is found exclusively in God. The only way we can get it is for Him to share His holiness with us (to impart it to us). That is the best thing that could ever happen to a human being. There is no greater gift than to "share in his holiness."

True, God's discipline is not always a pleasant experience. Sometimes it can be painful, like the surgeon's scalpel that is used to restore physical health. The only motive God has is to shepherd us into the place where He can share His holiness with us. It may involve giving up some unholy things that are incompatible with His holiness. "Sharing" in His holiness means letting His holiness become a part of us. It is literally merged into our cleansed human nature.

The final result of being trained by His discipline is a "harvest of righteousness and peace." Once again we see the wonderful results of God's plan for His people. Isn't God good!

We should appreciate and be thankful for God's discipline "because the Lord disciplines those he loves, and he punishes everyone he accepts as a son" (v. 6).

Question for Reflection: How has God disciplined you?

83

The Final Requirement

Make every effort to live in peace with all men and to be holy; without holiness no one will see the Lord.
—Heb. 12:14

The Bible contains many passages that are written as different forms of literature. There is poetry in the Psalms and elsewhere. Many of the Old Testament books are historical narratives. Jesus told fictional stories called parables, and Paul wrote letters. Some portions of the Bible may seem difficult to understand and require careful interpretation; however, others are exceedingly clear. This verse from Hebrews is an example. It deals with a vital principle, and it states that principle in terms that are absolute and clear. Without holiness, no one will see the Lord.

We understand "seeing God" to mean entering the place of His eternal abode. This preparation is the principal purpose for life in this world. What is the basic requirement for getting to see God?

It is expressed in such clear, simple terms that it is unmistakable, even to a child. There is just one thing that is absolutely indispensable. Without it there will be no entry into the presence of God. It is holiness!

It is evident that God's original purpose in creation was to enjoy a relationship of love, harmony, and fellowship with humankind. It can only happen where there is an absence of fundamental conflict. God created us that way, but our rebellion and disobedience introduced conflict and separation from God. The only way the situation can be reversed is for us to regain a likeness to God—to share a common nature with Him that eliminates conflict.

The object of every action God has taken in redemption is to open the door for the restoration of the original relationship. His plan is to create a new race with which He can have fellowship forever in heaven.

One thing is certain: nothing sinful will ever make it into heaven. No pleading, no excuses, no bargaining, no regrets, no tears, or anything else will get you past the pearly gates if you do not have a pure heart. A sinful nature would soon ruin heaven, and God is not going to take that risk.

The same work of God that prepares us to live victoriously in this world also prepares us for the entrance exam into heaven.

Question for Reflection: Are you ready to see the Lord?

84

The Objective of Christ's Death

And so Jesus also suffered outside the city gate to make the people holy through his own blood.

—Heb. 13:12

Why did Christ die on the Cross? There may be many details we could cite, and some theological speculation. But this text cuts through all superficial matters and goes right to the heart of the matter: He died to "make the people holy." That is the bottom line! He purchased the right to do it by shedding His own blood. His cross is the center of the whole scheme of salvation.

There are various steps, stages, and actions by both God and human beings that make salvation a reality, but it is all about God's plan to make us holy. Holiness is the final goal of the plan from beginning to end. There is no full salvation until holiness of heart has been achieved. John declared, "The reason the Son of God appeared was to destroy the devil's work" (1 John 3:8). Until holiness has been restored, the work of the devil has not been destroyed.

In *The Message*, John Peterson translates God's words from Ezek. 20:12 as, "I . . . am in the business of making them holy" (TM). How true! That really is God's principal business.

Holiness was His original plan in creation. Though the plan was temporarily thwarted by sin, the door was opened to recreate us in His own image again, through the death of Christ.

The death of Christ brought with it many benefits, but the final objective was "to make the people holy."

Question for Reflection: Have you realized God's ultimate goal in sending His Son to die?

85

True Religion: Compassionate and Unpolluted

Religion that God our Father accepts as pure and faultless is this: to look after orphans and widows in their distress and to keep oneself from being polluted by the world.   —James 1:27

What makes some diamonds more valuable than others? There are a number of factors, including the size of the stone, the way it is cut, and its color. One of the most important determinants in the value of a diamond is its clarity. Some stones have inclusions, which are tiny bits of impurity. Sometimes visible to the naked eye, they affect the brilliance of the stone. The bottom line? A perfectly clear diamond, free from inclusions, is to be desired.

James, in defining the essence of our faith, identifies two factors that make it precious. First, true religion involves a compassionate lifestyle. It is motivated by love, but it must be practical. It is not just sentiment, but action. Second, it must include being freed and kept free from the pollution that surrounds us in this world.

Caring for orphans and widows represents the practice of the core values of Christianity: love, concern for others, and compassion. These things are not valid unless they are actually put into practice. Belief is more than subscribing to a creed. If the creed is based on truth, our belief of it must be validated by incarnating it into our lives.

But true religion is more than going around doing good things. It must also deal with the problem of the corruption (pollution or depravity of our nature). Pollution is anything that keeps something from being pure. If a container is labeled "pure water," it should mean that it contains nothing but pure water. If you put dirt into the container, it has been polluted and is no longer pure water.

Sin, in any form, is a pollutant to the human spirit. It degrades and contaminates. True religion, as God sees it, must avoid the things that pollute.

We are surrounded daily by all kinds of pollutants in this world that constantly put us under pressure to open up to them. They come at us from every angle and sometimes are cleverly disguised to deceive us. We must be constantly vigilant to keep ourselves from being polluted by the world.

Question for Reflection: Are there "inclusions" remaining in your heart?

86

Double-Mindedness

Submit yourselves, then, to God. Resist the devil, and he will flee from you. Come near to God and he will come near to you. Wash your hands, you sinners, and purify your hearts, you double-minded.

—James 4:7–8

When standing at the altar to be married, there is only one good answer to the question "Will you have this woman to be your wedded wife?" That answer is "Yes!" Any hesitation or equivocation would spell doom for the intended union. "Sure, I guess so," is not what the bride wants to hear. When it comes to marriage, one is committed fully or not at all.

When submitting ourselves to God, the same principle applies. Double-mindedness will not do. James probably remembered from his own previous experience what the problem was like, but in trying to describe it he had to invent a new word, "double-minded." He used it twice in this Epistle, but it is not found anywhere else in the Bible. This word describes the person who is torn between two strong desires. He has the desire to love, serve, and be faithful to God, but at the same time there is something that is contrary to God and rises up to oppose the first desire. Paul put it this way: "When I want to do good, evil is right there with me. For in my inner being I delight in God's law; but I see another law at work in the members of my body, waging war against the law of my mind and making me a prisoner of the law of sin at work within my members. What a wretched man I am!" (Rom. 7:21–24).

Double-mindedness means instability, divided loyalties, and a constant internal conflict. But there is a two-step remedy: Sinners need to "wash their hands" of their guilt, and the double-minded need purification of a contrary-to-God nature.

The goal is to become single-minded, which means to live with a single purpose: to love and serve God without competition, to have only one supreme desire to glorify Him, to give attention to being faithful, and to have a heart purified from all competing loyalties. This is the cure for the "split personality."

This is purification from a sinful nature that opposes God. Once this problem is solved, the competition will cease and life will be lived with single purpose and a single focus.

Question for Reflection: Do you have any hesitation or reservation about submitting your whole self to God?

87

The Reason for It All

But just as he who called you is holy, so be holy in all you do; for it is written: "Be holy, because I am holy."
—1 Pet. 1:15–16

Good things usually take a little time. A good meal may take hours to prepare. A good education can be years in the making. And holiness—your sanctification—has been centuries in the making. In fact, it has been God's plan from the beginning.

This text answers some of the most important questions regarding God's redemptive plan: What is the final objective? What is the reason behind God's command that we be holy? It is not a distinctively New Testament concept, for it first appeared in the Book of Deuteronomy. God made it very clear from the beginning of the revelation of His plan for humankind what His reasons were. It took a long time for the plan to be worked out in its fullness, but the reason and the objectives never changed across the centuries.

In one simple statement God makes it clear what His desire for us is: He wants us to be holy! No alternatives are mentioned. Nothing less will ever please God. Everything God has done in our behalf has been directed toward reaching the goal of holiness. Beginning with creation, and then on through the Law, the Prophets, Calvary, and Pentecost, it has all had the purpose of leading us to personal holiness.

But a key question is, Why does He want us to be holy? Does He take any pleasure in a tyrannical domination of us? Is He seeking simply a form of harsh and cruel, degrading slavery? No, no, no! A thousand times no. Those answers miss the point entirely. God wants us to be holy because He is holy, and He wants to have a holy relationship with each one of us.

There are two reasons for His desire. (1) He wants us to be like Him so we can enjoy fellowship together. The intimate fellowship He seeks can only happen where all conflict has ceased. That is when we share the same interests, motives, and natures. (2) He loves us so much He desires the best for us. He knows what is best. There is nothing better than holiness. He knows that only holiness will lead us to a life of maximum blessing and satisfaction.

He wants to be good to us, and that is the reason He wants us to be holy. God could never desire anything better than that for us. We should never fear His plan but earnestly seek it.

Question for Reflection: How diligent are you right now about seeking holiness?

88

Participation in the Divine Nature

His divine power has given us everything we need for life and godliness through our knowledge of him who called us by his own glory and goodness. Through these he has given us his very great and precious promises, so that through them you may participate in the divine nature and escape the corruption in the world caused by evil desires.   —2 Pet. 1:3–4

Children usually resemble their parents. Sometimes the resemblance is not physical but can be seen in the attitude, behavior, or mannerisms of the child. A father and son may have the identical gait. A daughter's voice may sound so much like her mother's that it's difficult to tell them apart. Traits from one have been inherited by the other. Would you believe that you can come to resemble the God who created you, that you can actually have some share of His divine nature?

God has expressed what He wants to do for us in the "very great and precious" promises He has made in His Word. If we accept and act on these blessings, we will experience the incredible blessing, which Peter describes as "participat[ing] in the divine nature." What does this mean?

Holiness exists only in God. There is no other place where it can be found except in those to whom He imparts it. There is no other source. Holiness is the word that best describes God's nature. How is it possible for me to participate in His nature? Well, it takes a miracle! God literally takes the essence of His nature and imparts it to our heart. It can then be said that we share the same nature. It is truly a transforming miracle for the old sinful nature to be changed into godliness.

Peter goes on to say that through this act of God we will "escape the corruption in the world." The divine nature is pure. It is untouched by corruption and is completely uncontaminated by anything unholy. Before the divine nature can be imparted, all unholiness must be cleansed. This is how we escape the corruption in this world.

To participate in the divine nature means to have the mind of Christ: to think as He thinks, to see things through His eyes, to feel compassion as He feels it, to love as He loves, and to be moved by the things that move Him. To participate in the divine nature means others should see Jesus in us. As God shares His nature with us, we will become like Him.

Question for Reflection: In what way do you most resemble your Heavenly Father?

89

Make Every Effort

So then, dear friends, since you are looking forward to this, make every effort to be found spotless, blameless and at peace with him.   —2 Pet. 3:14

Occasionally you may notice that a neighbor has placed an item of value at the side of the road with a sign reading "Free." The old dresser, lawnmower, or second-hand bicycle is free for the taking. Anyone can have it. But not everyone does. Only the person who makes the effort to stop and pick it up will take home the treasure.

Likewise the provisions for our full salvation are a done deal. They are totally adequate and are available now! God has taken the initiative and has completed the provisions for His plan. At this point there is nothing that needs to be added. However, that does not mean that the plan will function automatically. It takes human cooperation with God to make it effective.

The operative phrase in this text is "make every effort." Of course, we understand that salvation comes by faith alone.

There is nothing we can do to deserve it. But that does not mean that it does not require any human effort.

It takes some effort to seek holiness. It requires patience and persistence to meet the requirements. Resisting temptation requires vigilance and firmness of resolve. Obedience may not always be easy. (Just ask Abraham about how he felt when God asked him to sacrifice his son Isaac.) Fulfilling God's call may mean sacrifice. God has never said that the Christian life will always be a bed of roses. It sometimes requires effort.

The good part is that adequate resources for success are always available. The promise is that God will never allow us to be tempted beyond what we can bear. God will never ask anything impossible. He will always give us the strength to accomplish what He asks us to do. Paul testified, "I can do everything through him who gives me strength" (Phil. 4:13).

If we do our part, God will always do His part. He will give us wisdom when we ask for it. Our victory over sin is assured.

Since we are looking forward to the wonderful things God wants to do for us, it will certainly be worth it to "make every effort" to keep ourselves "spotless, blameless and at peace with him."

Question for Reflection: What is your part in securing your holiness? Are you doing it?

90

Cleansing Through the Blood

> But if we walk in the light, as he is in the light, we have fellowship with one another, and the blood of Jesus, his Son, purifies us from all sin.   —1 John 1:7

It is often said that oil and vinegar don't mix. That isn't true, however. The two can be mixed for a short time.

Together, they make a lovely salad dressing! Light and darkness, on the other hand, absolutely cannot coincide. The very absence of light, by definition, makes darkness. They are opposites.

In the Bible light represents righteousness and darkness symbolizes evil. "God is light; in him there is no darkness at all" (v. 5). If we want to have fellowship with Him, we must walk in the light, for that is where He is. If God is light and we walk in the light, it signifies that we are in harmony with Him. Light and darkness are incompatible. When light comes, darkness is dispelled. The previous verse says that if we claim to have fellowship with God but walk in darkness, it is a lie.

Purity of heart is inseparable from fellowship with God. God cannot fellowship with darkness. But while we walk in fellowship with God, the blood of Christ purifies us from all sin. (Note the word "all," which indicates a complete, in-depth work of cleansing.) This is a great benefit and blessing, which was purchased for us by the blood of Jesus. To walk in the light, to have fellowship with God, and be purified from all sin should be primary goals for every Christian. These are the provisions God has made for us at great cost. We should not take them lightly. Changing their potential into reality should be the highest priority for all believers.

How sad it is to see people living below the full potential of what Christ's blood has purchased for us. God's plan of salvation is full, complete, and glorious. It meets every human need. It is all about having fellowship with God. He wants to remove every barrier to a rich, full enjoyment of His presence.

Walking in the light (obedience) is the key to fellowship. If we have the habit of obeying God, it will inevitably lead us to heart purity. That is because God wants us to have pure hearts, and He will lead us to it if we follow His directions. The only way you can miss heart holiness is deliberately not to seek it. "Seek and you will find" applies to holiness. If you want it bad enough, you can have holiness of heart.

Question for Reflection: Are you taking every step in the light?

91

Forgiveness and Purification

If we confess our sins, he is faithful and just and will forgive us our sins and purify us from all unrighteousness.   —1 John 1:9

A popular laundry detergent is marketed based on the fact that it performs a double action—it cleans and brightens. This product, its makers say, not only removes dirt from clothes but also leaves the colors even brighter and more vivid than before. It performs two actions at once. God's grace is like that. It both pardons and cleanses sins.

Sin is a twofold problem: (1) Sins as acts of disobedience committed against God. (2) Sin as an inbred principle or nature. A twofold problem requires a twofold solution. The first part of the problem requires forgiveness. The second part requires cleansing. It is interesting how, when speaking of full salvation, it mentions both of these together.

In the classic text above, it will be noticed that it speaks of forgiveness of sins and purification from unrighteousness.

In James 4:8, sinners are commanded to wash their hands and the double-minded are commanded to purify their hearts.

On the Day of Pentecost, those who were moved by Peter's message asked him what they needed to do. Peter replied, "Repent and be baptized, every one of you, in the name of Jesus Christ for the forgiveness of your sins. *And* you will receive the gift of the Holy Spirit" (Acts 2:38, emphasis added).

There are other examples in some of the classic Christian hymns:

"Rock of Ages," sung by a good part of the evangelical church, includes this phrase: "Let the water and the blood, / From thy wounded side which flowed, / Be of sin the *double cure*, / Save from wrath, and make me pure" (emphasis added).

"The Old Rugged Cross," perhaps the most well-known hymn in Christendom, says in verse 3, "For 'twas on that old Cross Jesus suffered and died, / To pardon *and sanctify* me" (emphasis added).

There are many more. It makes one wonder if those who sing these hymns realize they are singing Wesleyan theology.

Question for Reflection: Have you been cleansed from the carnal nature or only forgiven for your sins?

92

Purity like Christ's

Dear friends, now we are children of God, and what we will be has not yet been made known. But we know that when he appears, we shall be like him, for we shall see him as he is. Everyone who has this hope in him purifies himself, just as he is pure.

—1 John 3:2–3

If you have attended a high school or college reunion, you have probably marveled at how much certain people have changed. Some have perhaps gained weight. Others have gone bald or grown taller or begun wearing eyeglasses. After 15 or 20 years, none of us looks the same.

In spiritual terms, that's good news! In fact, we are changing for the better, being made more and more like Christ. When we have our grand reunion with Him, we will be amazed at how much we have changed to resemble Him.

There are still a lot of mysteries about our future life after death, but the apostle John is quite sure of some things. For example, when we see Him "we shall be like him." This has been the lifelong quest of many Christians. John testifies that it will be a reality when we see Jesus.

He goes on to say that everyone who has this hope purifies himself, "just as he is pure." What an amazing statement! Our purity will be just like His. Is that surprising? It really shouldn't be if we realize that our likeness to God has been the objective of the whole redemptive plan. Our purity and God's purity are very similar. That is what makes God's plan so great. Because we are alike, God can enjoy us, and we can enjoy God. There will be a real affinity between our natures. Our hearts will be attracted to the heart of God. God will want to fellowship with us because we are united in heart and spirit. This unity will be based on the fact that God is holy, and though we were sinful, we have been made holy just like He is. It will be the theme of our praise throughout eternity.

From this world our view of the next world, at best, is only like seeing "through a glass, darkly" (1 Cor. 13:12, KJV). But then, when the scales have been removed from our eyes, true reality will come into view and we will "see him as he is." We will contemplate His full glory as never before, which will give us even more reason to praise and glorify Him forever. It is good to know that we will no longer have to be in a hurry. All eternity will be ahead, which is how long we will need to adequately express our praise for the wonders of salvation.

To seek for purity is noble, but to raise the aspiration to seek for purity just as He is pure seems to add a special dimension.

Question for Reflection: In what way are you now becoming more like Christ?

93

The Devil's Work Destroyed

He who does what is sinful is of the devil, because the devil has been sinning from the beginning. The reason the Son of God appeared was to destroy the devil's work.
—1 John 3:8

Jesus declared that the reason for His coming was to destroy the works of the devil, and that victory has been ultimately secured in spite of the fact that we continue to deal with sin. The devil had succeeded in bringing the curse of sin on the human race. He had separated humankind from God, had brought the world under the rule of evil, and in general had made a mess of things in the world. But his success would only be temporary. God had a plan of redemption, which included sending His Son "to destroy the devil's work."

The devil's work began in the Garden of Eden where he sowed rebellion against God in the hearts of Adam and Eve and caused them to be expelled.

The devil is responsible for all the consequences of the original sin, including the sinful nature of human beings with which we are all born. The devil's work includes all of the sorrow, sickness, violence, and pain in the world today.

Jesus came with a plan to reverse everything the devil had done—to undo it. The battle was fought on the Cross. At last, the devil was defeated! When Jesus exclaimed, "It is finished!" the battle was over. The door had been opened again to complete victory over sin in all of its forms. We can now be delivered from the slavery of sin. The works of the devil were destroyed. Hallelujah! It is a glorious triumph. Jesus brought back what the devil took away.

Through the victory of Jesus we are invited back to the forgiveness of our sins and the purification of our hearts. The barriers to fellowship with God are removed. The doors of heaven are reopened.

Question for Reflection: Are you ready to claim your victory in Christ?

94

What Will Be Missing in Heaven?

> Nothing impure will ever enter it, nor will anyone who does what is shameful or deceitful, but only those whose names are written in the Lamb's book of life. —Rev. 21:27

How do you envision heaven? We usually think of heaven as being a wonderful place because of the things that will be there: the pearly gates, the golden streets, the jeweled walls, the crystal sea, our loved ones who have preceded us, and of course, Jesus himself. However, the glory of heaven will be seen by a few things that will be missing.

Heaven will be wonderful because nothing impure will ever be allowed to enter it. There will be nothing there that could ever contaminate it: nothing shameful or deceitful. Everyone in heaven will have a pure heart. Love will reign supreme. Can you imagine living in a society like that?

We will never have to fear terrible acts of terrorism again. We will never have to fear being mugged or robbed. The fact is, we will never have to be worried about anything bad ever happening to us because sin will be banished forever. God's plan will have come to its completion in a holy race of people. His will shall be perfectly done in all things.

This is a glorious hope, but it is also a solemn warning. Do you plan to be there? You are certainly invited, but there is a price to pay: you must be cleansed from all sin. No exceptions will be made; no excuses will be acceptable. If God should allow a sinful heart into heaven, it would no longer be heaven.

Ample provisions have been made, and ample time has

PUTTING THE PIECES TOGETHER

been given for you to get ready. If you do not make it, it will be your responsibility alone. "Blessed are the pure in heart, for they will see God" (Matt. 5:8). No other arrangement has been made.

If you miss heaven, you will have missed the final purpose of your entire life. Whatever causes you to miss it, you will regret it forever. It is far too important to ever think of delaying or neglecting it.

Question for Reflection: What in your life could possibly cause you to miss the blessing of heaven?

95

Eternity: A Continuation of Life

Let him who does wrong continue to do wrong; let him who is vile continue to be vile; let him who does right continue to do right; and let him who is holy continue to be holy.   —Rev. 22:11

How do you react when you see the red flashing lights of a police car in your rearview mirror? Most people, even if they are not speeding, feel a bit of tension. "Oh no," they wonder, "could he possibly be after me?" In the same way, some Christians feel tension about the prospect of the coming Judgment Day, even though they have been pardoned and cleansed from sin. Far from bringing tension, this thought should be a relief to those who are in Christ. The Great Judgment Day will not involve any significant change in us; it will be more a recognition of the spiritual achievement we have reached on earth and a continuation of it.

Those who have been doing wrong will go to hell where they can continue to do wrong. (There are no rules against it in hell.) If that has been their choice in life, it will continue to be their choice after life.

Those who are vile in life will continue their preferred lifestyle on the other side as well. If you have identified yourself with worldly values and worldly people, God must assume that those are the values and the people you want to continue with in eternity.

The same principle applies to righteous and holy people. Those who have achieved holiness of heart and life in this world will simply continue in the same lifestyle after the judgment.

The interesting thing is that the same choices that prepare us to live well in this world also prepare us for the world to come. Sanctifying grace is what makes us victorious in this life; it is the same grace that makes us victorious in the next life.

In effect, God says to us, "Make your choice. But be aware that it is a double choice. It will be in effect during your lifetime, but it will also extend through eternity." If you are holy when God calls you to account, you will continue to be holy. If you are not holy at that point, there is no longer any hope. The time for making choices has run out. Holiness in this life leads to holiness in heaven. There are no shortcuts.

Question for Reflection: Are you looking forward to eternity?

Afterword

Holiness is more than a doctrine to be believed: it is an experience to be received so that we can live out God's plan. Now that you have seen the biblical truth that it is God's will for us to be sanctified—to be holy—we fervently hope and pray that this experience will become a reality in your life. While it is important to understand this doctrine, it is more important to seek it and to have it become your personal experience. If you believe that you have experienced the infilling of the Holy Spirit before reading this book, we hope you have come to a deeper and more meaningful understanding of holiness.

If, on the other hand, this writing has opened to you a new vision of what God's grace can accomplish in your life, do not let it stop there. Seek holiness with all your heart! No matter what it costs, or how long it takes, hunger and thirst after it until the fullness of the Spirit becomes a mighty reality in your heart. Never accept less than the best that God has to offer you.

O God, please work in the heart of every reader, leading him or her to a full surrender to You and to the blessing of a heart made pure and holy by the work of Your Spirit. Amen.